2004

HARMONIC RHYTHM

HARMONIC RHYTHM

ANALYSIS AND INTERPRETATION

Joseph P. Swain

OXFORD

UNIVERSITY PRESS

2002

OXFORD
UNIVERSITY PRESS

Oxford   New York

Auckland   Bangkok   Buenos Aires   Cape Town   Chennai
Dar es Salaam   Delhi   Hong Kong   Istanbul   Karachi   Kolkata
Kuala Lumpur   Madrid   Melbourne   Mexico City   Mumbai   Nairobi
São Paulo   Shanghai   Singapore   Taipei   Tokyo   Toronto

and an associated company in Berlin

Copyright © 2002 by Oxford University Press

Published by Oxford University Press, Inc.
198 Madison Avenue, New York, New York 10016

www.oup.com

Oxford is a registered trademark of Oxford University Press

Library of Congress Cataloging-in-Publication Data
Swain, Joseph Peter.
Harmonic rhythm : analysis and interpretation / Joseph P. Swain.
p.   cm.
Includes bibliographical references and index.
ISBN 0-19-515087-2
1. Harmonic analysis (Music)   2. Musical meter and rhythm.   I. Title.
T50 .S955 2002
781.2'56—dc21   2001046496

1 3 5 7 9 8 6 4 2

Printed in the United States of America
on acid-free paper

PREFACE

$\mathcal{D}$ OES THE timing of harmonic changes affect our experience of a passage of music? Does it matter if chords progress from one to the next quickly or slowly?

These questions are rhetorical, of course. It is beyond doubt that the rhythm of harmonic changes has a great deal to do with the effects of those changes, that a composer's decision about when to alter a chord can count as much as the choice of what that new chord should be. Harmonic rhythm is one of the great resources of the Western musical tradition.

Explicit thinking about harmonic rhythm is a comparatively recent development in that tradition. Walter Piston first articulated the concept in 1941, but his followers' attempts to apply the idea in criticism foundered for lack of a consistent method of applying his concept, a theory of harmonic rhythm.

This book presents such a theory. Part I shows how to construct an analytical graph, called a dimensional analysis, of the harmonic rhythm of any passage. The dimensional analysis can be likened to a chemist's spectrograph of a compound: it isolates each of the components of harmonic rhythm, each harmonic aspect that changes, so that all may be evaluated separately yet seen together at a glance. Part II lays out a theory of interpretation of these graphs, which includes three simple postulates about musical tension, some illustrations of how to apply the method to nontraditional harmony, and some short criticism of five passages showing how this theory of harmonic rhythm can supplement the perspectives of other traditional approaches. The postulates have to do with fundamental musical perceptions and are supported, as are many other points throughout the book, by research from cognitive science and music psychology. In that aspect, I suppose, dimensional theory might be regarded as a perceptual theory, but that does not mean in the slightest that it is not an analytical theory of music as well. Indeed, any music theory that aims at the explanation of musical experience as its principal goal must be a perceptual theory.

The book requires no specialized knowledge beyond a good familiarity with traditional harmony and the Western musical tradition. In fact, because dimensional analysis draws on all the principal concepts of traditional harmony, an analysis in harmonic rhythm has proven to be an excellent capstone project at the end of an undergraduate harmony course here at Colgate University.[1] Therefore, although the book is written primarily for other musicologists and not as a textbook, I have kept student readers in mind, and I beg the indulgence of my colleagues if certain familiar topics such as compound melody or harmonic embedding receive a more leisurely treatment than would otherwise be warranted.

The book depends on a rather small number of musical examples that are visited again and again as the method is developed. The historical range runs from Machaut to Debussy. Some might wish for a greater range and more variety, but the main purpose here is to present a practical method of analyzing and interpreting harmonic rhythm, not to survey every contingency or illustrate what might happen in every kind of musical language. In theory, the method can analyze any passage, but the usefulness of the results will depend on the harmonic characteristics of the music under study. I depend on my colleagues who find the method promising to test its limits and usefulness in their own work and to propose improvements.

I have formatted the musical examples with Dr. Keith Hamil's Notewriter 2.88 software. I have tried to record every detail of the original scores that matters to harmonic analysis but not necessarily their every nuance, and I have reduced scores where possible to save space and to make the attending graphs easier to read.

I would like to thank the editors of *Music Theory Spectrum* for encouraging this enterprise at an early stage when they published in 1998 my article "Dimensions of Harmonic Rhythm," an outline of the main ideas. I thank also the good offices of Oxford University Press and especially their three anonymous reviewers, who made many helpful suggestions. Most of all I thank the composer Dr. Matthew Marullo, who read the manuscript and all the examples with great care, and three talented Colgate undergraduates who each spent a summer learning about harmonic rhythm, creating analyses, and formatting many graphs, a few of which turned into illustrations for this book: Jonathan Lee, Jason Haberman, and Heidi Hayes.

To my wife and family I am most grateful for the things that make one happy in life and, from time to time, for playing music with me.

Hamilton, New York
2001

CONTENTS

HARMONIC RHYTHM

CHAPTER I.

INTRODUCTION

*W*HAT IS harmonic rhythm? Imagine a pianist who plays the first phrase of "The Star-Spangled Banner" in the right hand and accompanies it with precisely the same chord for each beat in the left hand. Then imagine the melody accompanied by a different chord for each beat (see ex. 1-1). The notes in the second version are no faster than in the first; all the durations are the same. Yet the second seems far more active, with a forward motion entirely lacking in the first version.

In a more sophisticated contrast in harmonic rhythm, from one of George Frederic Handel's most famous choruses (ex. 1-2), we again perceive a motion that belies the evidence of the notes on the page. The first passage has rapid sixteenth notes; the second does not, yet for the listener the second seems faster somehow. More precisely, in some respects it presents more musical events or articulations per measure and thereby builds tension toward the great moment of arrival—"Wonderful, counsellor"—for which this piece is justly celebrated.

The cause of these perceptions is obvious. Although the notes do not move faster in the latter examples, and indeed in Handel's case they move more slowly, the chords change more quickly, and that makes all the difference. In the national anthem there is no change of triad at all, so the difference in the two versions is almost comic because the first sounds so wooden. In the chorus, the triads in the second passage change at twice the rate of the first, but that is enough to invigorate the sense of motion and heighten the mood from calm gladness to some sense of urgency

3

Ex. 1-1. Two different harmonizations of the opening phrase from "The Star-Spangled Banner."

leading to triumph. The perception of rhythm in general depends on the perception of changes in some musical phenomenon—pitch, articulation, instrumentation, any discrete change will do. Harmonic rhythm is simply that perception of rhythm that depends on changes in aspects of harmony.

"Possibly no single factor has so much importance in the achievement of good harmonic writing as rhythm," writes the composer Roger Sessions.[1] Harmonic rhythm is a tremendous musical resource, a powerful weapon in a composer's arsenal of structural and expressive effects. If musical in-

Ex. 1-2. Handel, "For unto us," no. 12 from *Messiah*, mm. 20–22, 26–28.

tuition does not make this plain, examples like those cited, which could be multiplied by the thousands, should make it so. After all, the harmonic element is arguably the most sophisticated aspect of the Western musical tradition. The timing of changes in that element and their coordination with other features of composition must constitute some of the most important choices a composer makes, conscious or not, and the most important perceptions molding the experience of the listener. Music in its essence is perceived and conceived motion, and most Western music comprises harmonic motion. The significance of harmonic rhythm follows from the most distinctive quality of the tradition.

A BRIEF HISTORY OF THE
CONCEPT "HARMONIC RHYTHM"

Harmonic rhythm was born the twin of polyphony. As soon as there was a vertical, or simultaneous, element to pitch organization—in short, when chords became an essential part of Western music—composers could make changes in chords that were to some extent independent of melody. Now it is true that the importance of harmonic rhythm as a musical resource is proportional to the degree of that independence. With the stricter kinds of medieval organum, in which the added organal voice moved precisely with the principal voice at a fixed interval, every harmonic aspect changes coincidentally with the changes in the melody. Only when the chant repeats tones, thus repeating the chord, does harmonic rhythm gain distinction, so in parallel organum the independence is very small indeed. But when composers conceived of polyphonic voices that could have rhythms independent of one another, probably at St. Martial in the twelfth century, then the organal voice could move at speeds different from the voice holding the chant melody, and the two voices together could set up a series of changes in the music—those moments when both voices change pitch at the same time—that is truly independent of the motions of the individual voices.[2]

Changing the harmony in its various aspects must have been one of the chief rhythmic considerations of leading composers since the twelfth century, but explicit recognition of harmony's rhythmic powers appeared in theoretical writings only much later. The baroque composer Jean Philippe Rameau (1683–1764), the first to organize scattered concepts of dissonance treatment, habitual progressions, inversions, and other matters into a real theory of harmonic syntax, forbade "harmonic syncopation," or changing the triad on weak beats and not on the strong.[3] Later writers advised the same. But such rules merely recognized rather vaguely that harmonic changes interacted with meter in some way. The concept of harmonic

rhythm as a significant theoretical entity that exerts more general and powerful musical effects had to wait until the mid–twentieth century, when the
composer Walter Piston began to teach it.[4]

In 1944 Piston presented this definition of harmonic rhythm to the musical world:

> Harmonic rhythm. The rhythmic life contributed to music by means of
> the underlying changes of harmony. The pattern of the harmonic rhythm
> of a given piece of music, derived by noting the root changes as they
> occur, reveals important and distinctive features affecting the style and
> texture.[5]

In these few words Piston transformed a vague supposition of the importance of harmonic change into a specific concept that has not seen serious
revision since. The key points of the definition are the two emphases on
change as the source of rhythmic perception and on root movements as
the locus of those changes. For Piston, the pioneer theoretician of harmonic
rhythm, changes in triads are the heart of the matter.

He brought out this essential point more clearly and at greater length
in his chapter "Harmonic Rhythm" in the first edition of his classic text
Harmony, published in 1941.[6] After pointing out the different speeds of the
various contrapuntal lines in a Beethoven minuet (ex.1-3), Piston deduces
the harmonic rhythm of the whole texture by writing down how many
beats each triad lasts before the next one in the progression replaces it.
Once the Roman numeral analysis has been made, the derivation of the
harmonic rhythm is completely straightforward. There is nothing to interpret except what the analysis means.

Ex. 1-3. Beethoven, Sonata op. 31, no. 2, III, mm. 13–16, printed as ex. 78 in *Harmony*, 1st ed., p. 43, followed by Piston's ex. 80, his analysis of the harmonic
rhythm.

Another eminent American composer, Roger Sessions, preserved Piston's concept intact in his own 1951 text on harmony, *Harmonic Practice*, and a rash of studies followed in the late 1950s and 1960s that sought to apply Piston's concept in the analysis of Bach, Mozart, Beethoven, and other masters.[7] Thereafter interest waned. Despite the promise of Piston's insight, two fundamental problems with it discouraged continuing analysis of harmonic rhythm in the late twentieth century.

WHY HARMONIC RHYTHM FAILED

The first problem arises from the nature of harmony itself: it is a phenomenon of many dimensions. Describing the rhythm of a melody can be a comparatively simple affair: measuring the time elapsed between the onset of one note and the onset of the next.[8] Piston tried to measure harmonic rhythm in an analogous way, by substituting the triad identities for notes of the melody, and that is why there can be no argument about the duration values of the harmonic rhythm, *once the Roman numeral analysis is set*. But music lovers can almost always find something to argue about in a Roman numeral analysis because harmony is a composite thing made of many elements interacting in complex ways. To see why this composite nature creates headaches for anyone who wants to analyze harmonic rhythm, let's reconsider Piston's analysis of Beethoven.

Piston writes "II" under the third beat of the first bar, but many other listeners would hear those Fs and A-flats and the C as a combination of passing and reaching tones. They understand the F minor triad as an accident of nonharmonic counterpoint, particularly since the E-flats in alto and bass hold through, constantly reminding the listener of I. Piston takes exactly this stance at the cadence in measure 16, hearing the F_5, A-flat$_4$, D$_4$ combination on the downbeat as various dissonant tones, rather than writing "V," which would account for all except the bass.

Erasing the "II" or adding the "V" changes the triad durations and therefore the analysis of the harmonic rhythm. Piston himself recognized this issue of the passing chord, as he called it, and advised careful consideration of the tempo to help one decide. But in the end, decide one must. There cannot be two mutually exclusive interpretations of the same phenomenon, even though it might well be possible for a single listener to hear it two ways.

And the passing chord problem is not the only headache. The particular root of a triad often affects the musical dynamic less than the chord's function. When Beethoven's harmony in the third bar passes from C minor to F minor (VI–II in Piston's symbols), it merely substitutes one subdominant function triad for another. The listener waits expectantly for the dominant meanwhile, which arrives on the third beat. Isn't it reasonable to think that the harmonic change of function from subdominant to dominant is more powerful, more salient, than the change of the individual triads?

What about that lovely F-sharp in bar 2? In triadic theory, it is a simple chromatic neighbor tone. But at the moment it sounds, the listener experiences a new harmony—a new simultaneous combination of tones. Does that experience of change count for nothing?

Beethoven initiates new triads with varying numbers of contrapuntal voices: sometimes three, sometimes two, and at the cadence, with only one, the bass. Does it matter that triads can change with more or less contrapuntal activity, more or less force?

It is easy to say that harmonic rhythm comes from the perception of changes in harmony, but when it comes to measuring them, what is to count as a "change in harmony"? What counts as a chord? There are many dimensions to every harmonic event, and it is this fact, more than anything else, that frustrated the efforts of Piston's followers. They had to simplify harmonic events down to one dimension—triad identity—in order to apply Piston's definition, and in the long run their simplifications were impoverishments, too personal and too idiosyncratic. The unfortunate and unavoidable impression was a lack of theoretical consistency and rigor.

Even this might have been excused had the studies of harmonic rhythm found new interpretations that, like all good criticism, could enlighten and amplify the listener's experience. But little in the way of durable results seems to come of them. Piston's concept of harmonic rhythm did not reveal any consistent principles or patterns or even insight into particular compositions, despite its obvious relevance to passages like Handel's. Moreover, because of its triadic orientation, only music built on functional harmony (common practice) appeared relevant, even though, all Western music since 1200, excepting some kinds of monophony but including the modernist and popular languages, has harmonic change built into its fabric. This, then, is the second of the major problems with Piston's concept: limited scope.

A REVIVAL OF HARMONIC RHYTHM

The dimensional analysis of harmonic rhythm presented in this book attacks both problems directly. The first part of the book recognizes the multidimensional quality of the harmonic event by teasing apart, one by one, its various dimensions and giving each its own analysis, much as a beam of light is diffracted into its various component colors. Example 1-4 shows what this diffraction looks like when complete.

Chapters 2 through 7 treat each kind of harmonic analysis, or dimension, one at a time, explaining what each one means and giving instructions for

Ex. 1-4. Beethoven, Sonata op. 31, no. 2, III, mm. 13–16, dimensional analysis.

deriving it. I begin at the top with textural rhythm and proceed downward. This order of execution is, I believe, the easiest way to arrive at the complete analysis, but, with the exception of density, each individual dimension is logically independent and may be derived directly from the score without having any of the others. In practice, contextual considerations of the hierarchically "lower" dimensions may indeed affect judgments about the "upper" ones. This is no circular reasoning but simply the inclusion of context in analytical judgment.[9] Whether all the dimensions are always necessary depends on the analytical question being asked. Experience has shown that the most interesting insights come from comparing the dimensions with one another.

That comparison goes far toward solving Piston's second problem of practicality. The second part of the book (chapters 8–12) discusses how to apply dimensional analysis to practical issues in analysis and criticism. It begins by presenting commonsense theoretical principles of interpretation that reflect aspects of our musical experience. These principles are the basis for interpreting the finished dimensional graphs.

It is remarkable that, during a period when the discipline of music theory has striven, for good or ill, for the precise kind of discourse characteristic of mathematics, that some basic technical terms still have varying usage. To prevent confusion and misunderstanding, the following list defines some common technical terms as they are used in this book.

> *chord*—any simultaneous sounding of different pitches (there is no presumption about intervallic content or structure)
>
> *contrapuntal texture*—a polyphonic texture of independent melodies of more or less equal salience
>
> *homophonic texture*—a polyphonic texture of one salient melody (the perceptual figure) and accompaniment (the perceptual ground)
>
> *melody*—any succession of pitches perceived as a continuous *Gestalt*, or "shape"
>
> *monophony*—a texture of one melody
>
> *pitch-class*—the set of all pitches related by whole number multiples of a fundamental frequency (e.g., "B-flat pitch class" includes all pitches named B-flat or A-sharp)
>
> *polyphony*—a texture of more than one melody (no degree of melodic independence is implied)
>
> *seventh chord*—triad with an additional factor created by the superimposition of one additional pitch-class at the interval of a third
>
> *texture*—the quality of simultaneously sounding melodies; this quality may be specified by a specific quantity (e.g., four-voice texture) or by more generic qualifiers (e.g. contrapuntal texture)
>
> *triad*—chord consisting of a root pitch-class and two factors made by superimposing two more pitch-classes at the intervals of a third and a fifth; the triad's name is taken from the root pitch-class
>
> *voice*—one melody of a polyphonic texture

The list leaves out the two most essential terms, "rhythm" and "harmony," and for good reason, since these concepts have acquired so many diverse usages and connotations that a one-line definition is foolhardy.[10] As noted, the essential aspect of rhythm behind this study is change in some musical aspect. Without a perceived discrete change, there can be no rhythm. Conversely, whenever a listener hears a discrete change in any aspect of music, there is rhythm. Harmony, at its most fundamental, arises when different pitches sound simultaneously. More broadly, harmony is a conception of the listener that takes in language-like pitch organizations, such as syntactic progression, expectation, and the sensation of musical tension, among many other things, so that harmony can be perceived even when only one pitch at a time is sounding, as in an Alberti bass. The theory of harmonic rhythm that follows—dimensional analysis—thereby describes and interprets the perceived changes in aspects of harmony of a musical composition.

Dimensional analysis is designed to help provide the musical insights and enlightened appreciation that Walter Piston sought with his pioneering concept. It should go without saying, however, that dimensional analysis will only rarely, if ever, provide the basis for a thorough understanding of any piece. Instead, its conclusions work better in concert with other modes of understanding the rich heritage of the Western tradition. Harmony is perhaps that tradition's richest feature, with its many dimensions, but it is only one feature. Still, harmonic rhythm, while ultimately indissoluble from music's other aspects, affects the listening experience essentially, as Handel and the national anthem do show. If these brief passages, short, simple, and even artificial as they are, make the point plainly, what of harmonic rhythm in more fulsome listening?

PART I.

Analysis of
Harmonic Rhythm

CHAPTER 2.

THE RHYTHM OF THE TEXTURE

*T*HE EVALUATION of rhythm relies heavily on relative comparison. Rhythmic events are faster or slower, of longer or shorter duration, metrically stronger or weaker, and so on. There is no theoretical limit to the parameters in most of these comparisons, although of course there may be practical limits. The evaluation of harmonic rhythm relies on such comparisons too, but there is a theoretical upper limit to its speed, its rate of change: the rhythm of its texture.

The texture of a piece of music has to do with the quality of the simultaneity of its melodies. Terms describing this quality inform us whether there are in fact simultaneous melodies—polyphony—or just one: monophony. Polyphonic textures are often further specified by the precise number of melodies, or voices, active in a given passage (e.g., "three-voice texture") and by the relations of those melodies. Polyphony having one predominant melody, as in a song, we call "homophony"; if more than one, "contrapuntal." Or texture may be specified further by citing a compositional technique, as in the Alberti bass, a harmonic character, as in "seventh-chord texture," or its orchestration, and as in "string texture," among many other distinctions.

Whatever kind of musical texture is at hand, its various melodies articulate rhythmic patterns by the durations of their notes. We perceive durations by noting the onsets, or attacks, of the notes since they mark precisely when the previous note has ended and a new one begun—a most fundamental kind of change that creates rhythm. In a polyphonic texture, of course, different melodies make onsets sometimes simultaneously, some-

Ex. 2-1. Example 78, showing Beethoven, Sonata op. 31, no. 3, III, mm. 13–16, and example 79, showing Piston's rhythmic analysis of the passage's four-voice texture.

times not. Walter Piston shows this point clearly in his very first discussion of harmonic rhythm. (ex. 2-1). Piston shows the rhythmic patterns of the four simultaneous melodies separately. Onsets of new notes sometimes line up; at other times, a single melody makes an attack alone. Never do all four melodies attack new notes at the same time.

Inasmuch as the rhythm of a single melody is conceived as the duration pattern of its pitches, the rhythm of a texture, by analogy, can be conceived as its pattern of durations within the texture, where duration is the length of time from any onset of a note anywhere in the texture to the next onset anywhere in the texture. In the example, it happens that there is a new attack by at least one of the four melodies every half beat, so the rhythm of its texture ("textural rhythm" from here on) is graphed by a string of eighth notes (ex. 2-2). Other writers have called this rhythm of an entire texture "composite rhythm" because a polyphonic texture is composed of simultaneous melodies and so in terms of melodies it is a composite, not an elementary, phenomenon.[1]

Properly speaking, textural rhythm is not harmonic rhythm at all, since by repeating a chord precisely, or even by repeating just one of its pitches,

Ex. 2-2. Textural rhythm of Beethoven, Sonata op. 31, no. 3, mm. 13–16.

Texture

there is a new attack that shows up in the textural rhythm, while there is no change of harmony in any aspect, and therefore no harmonic rhythm. Why, then, should we represent textural rhythm as one of the dimensions in a graph of harmonic rhythm? Having the textural rhythm at the top of the graph gives an absolute standard, a theoretical limit to the harmonic rhythm of the passage under analysis: no dimension of harmonic rhythm can possibly move faster than the textural rhythm at any moment. When it comes to judging how fast any particular dimension of harmonic rhythm moves, it is often useful to know exactly how fast it *could* move, if the composer so desired, within that texture.

It is quite simple to demonstrate the truth of this theoretical limit. Harmony arises when different pitches sound simultaneously to make a chord, and harmonic rhythm arises from changes in that chord. But any change means a new pitch, therefore a new attack on a note, and so occurs also in the rhythm of the texture. Therefore there can be no harmonic rhythm without a corresponding textural rhythm, but there can be textural rhythm without corresponding harmonic rhythm, as when a chord is precisely repeated. Therefore, the textural rhythm represents the maximum harmonic rhythm that could be employed by the composer for that passage.[2]

GRAPHING RHYTHM OF
THE TEXTURE

Graphing the textural rhythm means, in plain English, writing down the fastest-moving notes at every moment in the passage. Consider the opening of the Adagio movement from the "Christmas" Concerto of Arcangelo Corelli (ex. 2-3). The textural rhythm of the first measure is continuous sixteenth notes.[3] That is because the first solo violin has them for two beats, the second solo violin for two more, and no other instrument attacks new notes while a sixteenth-note value is sustained. In other words, the note-rhythms of the slower instruments subsume the sixteenth-note motion without subdivision. Sixteenths represent the maximum motion (or the shortest durations in the texture) throughout the first measure.

Sometimes the textural rhythm graph shows patterns that do not occur in any of the individual melodies. At the last beat of measure 2, for instance, the textural rhythm of one eighth and two sixteenths arises from the interaction of the two violin parts, or the cello and viola parts, which are coincident with them. And in measures 5 and 6 the two violin melodies alone create a series of suspensions and resolutions. Each part generally moves slowly, at durations of a quarter note, but because their attacks do not coincide, but rather alternate by half beats (eighths), the textural rhythm that they produce together is continuous eighths.

Ex. 2-3. Corelli, Concerto op. 6, no. 3, III, mm. 1–6.

Generally speaking, then, deriving the textural rhythm is a simple affair. There are just a few complications.

One complication occurs when the onset of a rhythmic event is not a new note, but a new rest, silence. Most times, rests in one voice of the texture are covered by pitch attacks in another voice. In measure 3 of example 2-3, it is the solo cello that gives the texture its pattern of continuous sixteenths. What about the sixteenth rest that starts every group in the sequence? It is not an issue, since the violins begin new notes every time that sixteenth rest occurs. But consider the conclusion of the rapid middle section of the same movement (ex. 2-4). Here Corelli writes quarter rests in all the parts, so there are periods of time without any new pitch attacks anywhere in the texture. But the silence itself is clearly a rhythmic event that deserves representation in the textural rhythm; otherwise, it wouldn't matter if the string players played half notes. But of course it does matter. Half notes would wreck the dramatic ending Corelli desires. In this case, it is not a pitch onset but the pitch cutoff of each chord that defines the beginning of the salient event. That is why it is an important and excellent effect for the musicians to execute cutoffs like this accurately and precisely together, for they contribute mightily to the rhythm of a passage.

The middle case of a rest occurring within a texture of sustained tones, without any coincidental note attack elsewhere, demands some judgment. The listener must decide whether the withdrawal of the resting voice is audible and thus creates a rhythmic event. In a two-voice texture of violin and bass (ex. 2-5), common in Handel's music, the cutoffs of the violins in measures 5 and 7 is certainly audible if the musicians make them precisely. There is certainly a change in the chord that the listener hears. In such cases, the rest should be treated like the onset of a new note.[4] But if the

Ex. 2-4. Corelli, Concerto op. 6, no. 3, III, mm. 18–21.

Ex. 2-5. Handel, "I know my Redeemer liveth," no. 45 from *Messiah*, mm. 1–8.

composer of a denser texture wants to give a singer a breathing space before beginning a long melody, the momentary withdrawal may not be perceptible. No discrete change need be recorded.

Another complication of textural rhythm is melodic ornamentation. In example 2-6, Bach has composed a violin solo that is heavily ornamented with mordents, grace notes, fussy rhythms such as the thirty-seconds in measure 2, and later on, trills.

Ornamentation poses two problems, one practical, the other theoretical. The practical matter that bears on graphing textural rhythm concerns the values given to the ornaments. The durations of ornamental notes have in many cases been controversial for centuries and in other cases are simply indeterminate. How long does the C-sharp$_5$ grace note last? Does it come before the strong beat or on it? Does the orchestra enter with the beginning of the mordent or after it? Are the durations of ornaments precise fractions of beats?

Ex. 2-6. J. S. Bach, "Erbarme dich," no. 47 from the *St. Matthew Passion*, mm. 1–2.

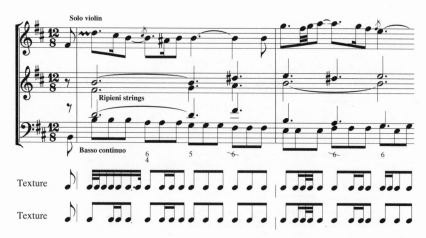

The theoretical question seems preposterous at first: is an ornament really a note? Ornaments are pitch events played by real instruments, and real instruments certainly play real notes. How could ornaments not be real notes? If music were merely a physical phenomenon—sound waves that strike the ear—then this argument would be conclusive, but music has a decisive conceptual dimension to it. Some writers would claim that music is entirely conceptual, existing wholly in the minds of listeners.[5] But there is no need to take such an extreme position. If music is even partly conceptual, then what the community of listeners *conceives of as notes*, and not just physical events, is quite relevant. The very notion of "ornamentation" suggests sounds that do not share the status of "real" notes that constitute the "real" melody. If this were not true, then trills and grace notes would not be called ornaments, but instead would be counted equally along with all the other notes of a melody. "Ornamentation" implies that listeners abstract a plainer version of the melody from the decorated version they perceive at first. If listeners do not conceive of ornaments as notes, then there is no pitch event to be graphed as part of the textural rhythm.

Bach does not make the decision easy in his violin melody. At one point he writes out the decoration (m. 2, beat 1) with all the precision his notation allows, a somewhat infamous feature of all his music, yet at other places he writes the grace notes, ornamental wild cards. So here is a case where slightly different analyses of the textural rhythm are valid and defensible, and example 2-6 includes two of them. The first treats all the ornaments as real notes and assigns them precise duration values, as controversial as they may be. The second analysis regards the conceptual violin melody as simpler and accordingly produces a simpler graph of the rhythm of the texture.

CHAPTER 3.

PHENOMENAL HARMONIC

RHYTHM

*T*HE FIRST real dimension of harmonic rhythm returns to fundamental assumptions. Harmonic rhythm in general is that perception of rhythm arising from changes in aspects of harmony. Harmony is simply a simultaneous sounding of different pitches; this creates the harmonic phenomenon or chord. So at its most fundamental, harmonic rhythm occurs whenever the pitch collection of any chord changes to create a new chord: this is phenomenal harmonic rhythm.

In the Bach prelude of example 3-1, the phenomenal harmonic rhythm moves at maximum speed, as fast as the textural rhythm. With every eighth-note beat, there is a new simultaneous pitch collection, a new chord: beat 1, A_3 and E_4; beat 2, A_3 and A_4; beat 3, E_3 and G-sharp$_4$, and so on. By contrast, Antonio Vivaldi chooses a very slow phenomenal harmonic rhythm to begin his "Winter" concerto. A new chord occurs only once every measure; the textural rhythm is eight times faster than the phenomenal.

Note that there has been no mention of triads here or any other kind of familiar or standard harmonic structure. The Vivaldi passage, in fact, has no pure triads, although we might easily infer some from the chords presented. Recording such inferences must await another dimension. Roots, harmonic functions, inversions, or any other structural consideration of the chord are quite irrelevant to the dimension of phenomenal harmonic rhythm. It is the most objective of all the dimensions in the sense that there are no judgments beyond those already made in graphing the textural rhythm.

Ex. 3-1. J. S. Bach, Prelude in A Major from *The Well-Tempered Clavier*, vol. 2, mm. 1–3; Vivaldi, Concerto op. 8, no. 4, "Winter," I, mm. 1–4.

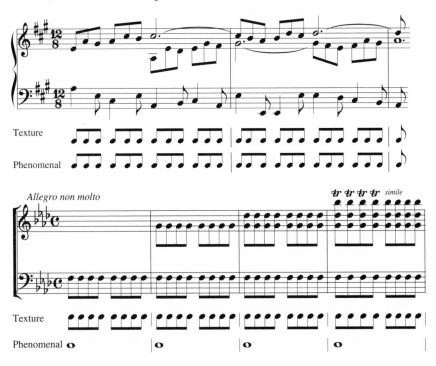

The phenomenal dimension is useful for at least two reasons. One is that the comparison of phenomenal rhythm with the textural may define an essential characteristic of a passage. It is very plain to the ear that the Bach has a lot of harmonic activity, but there is a serenity to that movement that proceeds from the unanimity of the textural and phenomenal rhythms. There is no conflict, no competition. The Vivaldi opening, on the other hand, conveys a rather mysterious nervousness, because it is strange to hear each dissonant chord reiterated so many times without any change. The speed of the texture suggests rapid motion, but the harmonic rhythm resists it, which, along with the dissonances piling up, creates a terrific strain.

A second reason derives from the objectivity of phenomenal rhythm. If anyone is interested in the harmonic rhythm of musical languages in which triads have no traditional functions, as in early Renaissance or medieval times, or in which there may be no triads at all, as in modern times, the dimension that treats all chords alike without discrimination can be the avenue of first approach.

GRAPHING

Graphing the phenomenal harmonic rhythm is quite straightforward. Any new or altered pitch creates a new harmonic phenomenon (chord), whose duration lasts until the next new pitch. Rests found in the textural rhythm graph transfer to the phenomenal, since they represent changes in chords. The only possible complication is the octave question.

What if, under a sustained chord, the bass leaps an octave? Or what if a composer simply reorders the pitches of a chord into different octaves, as often happens? Are these new chords, new harmonic phenomena, or simply reiterations?

The perceptual reality of the octave similarity is recognized all over the world, and the most familiar theory for western music, the Roman numeral triadic theory going back to Rameau, explicitly treats pitches related by one or more octaves—pitch-classes—as equivalent. If the constituent notes of a triad are transposed, there is no change in the analysis: the Roman numeral remains the same. Indeed, Rameau's insights into the nature of harmonic roots depend on treating octaves as pitch identities.[1] More recently, the linear analysis of Heinrich Schenker very often views the members of a pitch-class (e.g., all Ds) to be interchangeable, and pitch-set theory always does.

On the other hand, some theorists, such as Leonard Meyer, treat pitch-class members as different pitches. There is a great body of evidence showing that in the perception of melodies, listeners hear octave pitches quite distinctly.[2] One kind of experiment showed that when the notes of familiar tunes are transposed by octaves, listeners can no longer recognize the melodies.[3] In addition, a number of compositional cliches, such as the bass leaping down one octave from the dominant before resolving (5–5–1) indicate that the pitch change affects the chord somehow. The dimension of phenomenal harmonic rhythm therefore graphs octave pitches as distinct events; indeed, that partly explains the rhythmic effect of such cliches.

Some circumstances make it possible to abbreviate the graph of phenomenal harmonic rhythm. One is the surprisingly frequent occasion when the textural and phenomenal rhythms are identical throughout a passage, as they are in the Bach prelude of example 2-1. In this case a single line of notation with a double title is perfectly sufficient. The Chopin etude in example 3-2 shows another circumstance. Chopin constructs this beautiful piece around two principal melodies in the soprano and bass. He fills the space between them with a consistent shimmer of arpeggios. In the words of his friend Robert Schumann:

Ex. 3-2. Chopin, Etude op. 25, no. 1, mm. 1–3.

Imagine an Aeolian harp capable of all sonorous levels, and an artist's hand animating it, adding here and there all kinds of fantastic embellishments, always, however, with a strong bass audible and, in the treble, a softly flowing cantilena, and you have some idea of his playing. . . . It would be a mistake to suppose that he made all the small notes individually audible: it was more an undulation of the A-flat major chord, lifted here and there high up on the keyboard, with the help of the pedal.[4]

The design is reflected in his notation in the large and small noteheads. It so happens in this etude that the most salient harmonic rhythms move much more slowly than the textural or phenomenal, which participate not at all in the principal rhythmic and harmonic gestures of the movement. Chopin uses this rapid arpeggiation as a sonic backdrop against which the main action will play out, much like a painter who begins the canvas with a colored wash that will surround all the figures to be put thereon without being a part of them. Because it is so consistent, it seems a waste of space and a distraction from the main interest to insist on including the textural/ phenomenal graph at full value. Instead, we graph one measure in full to show the pattern and then abbreviate measures that preserve the soprano and bass melodies as originally notated, while indicating all the notes of the arpeggios. The voice-leading of the inner parts is clearer than in the original notation. No information is lost.

There may be other circumstances that demand abbreviation and other methods for doing so. In certain analyses it may be wise to dispense with the textural and phenomenal dimensions altogether, depending on the goals and creativity of the analyst.

CONTRAPUNTAL PHENOMENAL
HARMONIC RHYTHM

The Chopin passage and the beginning of the B-flat Piano Sonata, K. 333, of Mozart (ex. 3-3) have something in common with the Bach prelude (ex. 3-1): the phenomenal harmonic rhythm moves at maximum speed, completely coincident with the rhythm of the texture. The significance of this fact, however, is somewhat different in the Bach. There, every new pitch represents the movement of a voice in the texture, soprano, alto, or bass. Mozart and Chopin instead construct arpeggiated textures that represent the many voices by sounding one pitch at a time. The left hand in the first measure of Mozart's sonata, for example, presents the B-flat$_3$ for the bass voice, the D$_4$ for the tenor, and the F$_4$ for the alto, all the while sounding a single melody for them all. This is an illusion known as the compound melody, and it has been recognized in music theory for centuries.[5] The separate voices come in and out rapidly and create the impression of continuity, much as a flashing light board at a sports stadium can create the illusion of pictures while really being dark most of the time.

Ex. 3-3. Mozart, Piano Sonata in B-flat, K. 333, I, mm. 1–3, showing the derivation of the contrapuntal harmonic rhythm.

Ex. 3-4. Corelli, Concerto op. 6, no. 8, III, mm. 9–17.

So the coincidence of textural and phenomenal rhythm in Mozart and Chopin signifies a different compositional technique from its coincidence in Bach and creates a different impression in listening. To view the motion of contrapuntal *voices* in Mozart and Chopin, some abstraction away from the objective notation is required. This is contrapuntal phenomenal harmonic rhythm: the changes in harmonic phenomena caused by moving voices.

When the main (soprano) melody reaches B-flat$_4$ in the first measure of Mozart, it remains there for a duration of four eighths, or one half note. Meanwhile, the "bass" enters on B-flat$_3$ and stays there; the "tenor" on D$_4$; and the "alto" on F$_4$. When the texture is conceived in this way, for four virtual voices rather than two real ones, there is no change in the constitution of the four-voice chord for that half-note duration.[6] This pattern repeats with slight variation in the next two bars. Example 3-3 shows the derivation of the contrapuntal phenomenal harmonic rhythm for those measures. The analysis highlights one way that Mozart's main idea for the sonata emphasizes the weak beat. The contrapuntal phenomenal analysis of the Chopin, for its part, shows how much slower the movement of voices is than the surface texture, to say nothing of triads and functions. The arpeggiated figuration is indeed just a coloristic background.

Consider one more example from Corelli's Adagio (ex.3-4), the fast middle section of the movement. The score might not suggest any compound melodic writing, but good professional violinists can play that first part so rapidly that it is easy to believe that every pair of sixteenths sounds simultaneously, as a chord. Once again, the phenomenal harmonic rhythm is as fast as the textural, but the contrapuntal phenomenal harmonic rhythm is much different and reveals how the second violin generates singlehandedly the sense of acceleration felt as the section progresses. First, its main motive shortens from three (half-note) beats to two. Then, in the latter half, the repeated pitches that produced a comparatively slow contrapuntal rhythm from measures 9 through 13 give way to arpeggios (m. 14), driving the contrapuntal rhythm toward the harmonic resolution analyzed in chapter 2 (ex. 2-4).

The addition of the contrapuntal dimension is not to be taken lightly, for it requires new judgments that remove it from the completely objective phenomenal dimension. The analyst must decide first of all whether there is a compound melody present, and then, if there is at least one, what will count as a change of voice in this illusive counterpoint. Nevertheless, in the right circumstances this dimension can make important contributions to the analysis of harmonic rhythm.

CHAPTER 4.

BASS PITCH HARMONIC RHYTHM

*T*HE ALLEGRO middle section of Corelli's Adagio movement from his "Christmas" Concerto (ex. 4-1) would seem to
offer a textbook demonstration of how Walter Piston distinguished harmonic rhythm from melodic rhythm. The first violin flashes
with rapid sixteenths, and the other melodies drive with constant eighths,
but the triadic motion that most interested Piston is at the half note,
much slower. It is very easy to hear the two kinds of motion, since the
contrast is great and both motions are consistent. But not perfectly consistent.

On closer examination, the constancy of the half-note triadic motion
turns out to be a curious illusion. The C minor triad repeats in a new
disposition in measure 10, as does the E-flat major in measures 13–14. Why
then the false first impression? Why is it difficult to hear pauses in the
forward momentum of the harmonic rhythm? Because there is a very important harmonic element that does move with perfect half-note consistency, and that is the bass.

Throughout the so-called common practice period, when musical languages assigned specific syntactic roles or functions to different triads within
the context of a key, music theorists, analysts, and critics have pointed to
the bass voice of a texture as the one that has the most effect on harmonic
articulation and movement. German writers have called it *Harmonieträger*,
the harmony carrier. Since Rameau, harmonic analysis has focused on triad
identities, but many thinkers before him said nothing of triads but instead
wrote very useful books on how to build compositions on a bass line.[1]

Ex. 4-1. Corelli, Concerto op. 6, no. 8, III, mm. 9–14.

These are the famous thorough-bass methods, preferred by no less a teacher than Johann Sebastian Bach.

This historical emphasis on the harmonic priority of the bass voice makes a lot of sense. Acoustical science tells us that it is the lowest-sounding pitch, the fundamental, that determines the pitches of the other, higher partial frequencies, which some writers have cited to explain why the most stable chords are in root position. Indeed, the perceived strength of a chord's identity and its function derive partly from its inversion. The pitch of the bass has always remained conceptually distinct from the identity of the triad, and that allows the bass voice its melodic freedom; it is not entirely a slave to the chord progression. Changing the inversion of a triad is a harmonic change of some independence.

Corelli takes advantage of this independence. The first three half-note beats change both bass pitch and root, establishing a strong pattern. When

Ex. 4-2. Piston's reduction of Beethoven, Symphony no. 7, II, mm. 1–4, followed by his analysis of its harmonic rhythm.

A: I   V ------------   I

Harmonic rhythm

the bass leaps a full octave, the C root remains, but the listener, preferring consistency to interruption,[2] hears the gesture as one more half-note beat in the harmonic rhythm, a perception immediately reinforced by several more real root changes on the half-note beat before Corelli makes the same trick work again.

Walter Piston himself may have had some second thoughts about placing all the weight of harmonic rhythm on triad movement without an independent bass. Example 4-2 is his own analysis of the harmonic rhythm that begins the slow movement to Beethoven's Seventh Symphony.[3] By his own definitions and practice, the analysis should be: half note, whole note, half note, but that is not what he writes. The Roman numerals reflect the triad movements, but he preserves the bass line as a series of half notes, unwilling to omit that element's contribution to the harmonic perception. His fellow composer Roger Sessions wrote in his *Harmonic Practice* that "a change of [chord] position may sometimes become rhythmically equivalent to a real harmonic change; generally when this is true it is the result of a striking skip in the bass, or of some other kind of vigorous contrapuntal movement."[4] And how many times have we heard bass lines like that in a typical piano rag (ex. 4-3)? Thousands of marches, waltzes, and salon pieces are full of this "oom-pah" bass that gives the impression of a very active harmony while changing triads at a snail's pace. Composers in the nineteenth century, in particular, found this technique an easy way to stretch out harmonic functions over long phrases without too static an effect within the bar.

In short, the movement of a functional bass voice creates perceptions of changes in harmonic aspect. The dimension of the bass pitch rhythm captures this element of harmonic rhythm.

Ex. 4-3. Joplin, "The Entertainer," mm. 21–22.

Texture
Phenomenal

Bass pitch

GRAPHING

To graph the bass pitch rhythm, one must remember that it is not the duration of each written bass note, but the total duration of each bass pitch that counts. In the A Major Prelude (ex. 4-4), as in so much of Bach, the rhythm of the bass line is at first coincident with the rhythm of its pitch changes: every new bass note is a new pitch. But in the second measure, he sounds E_2 and then E_3 twice each. Whenever a bass pitch is reiterated, the analyst sums up all the iterations until there is a new pitch. In this case the sum is a dotted quarter note, expressed here instead with a tie to keep the meter clear to the eye. In the Corelli (ex. 4-1), the rhythm of the bass is clearly eighth notes, but only pitch changes can signal a change of harmonic aspect. The bass pitch rhythm is the sum of each group of four eighth notes, or one half note per change.

Ex. 4-4. J. S. Bach, Prelude in A Major from *The Well-Tempered Clavier*, vol. 2, mm. 1–2.

Texture
Phenomenal

Bass pitch

The second bar of the prelude brings up again the octave question. Do the leaps from E_3 to E_2 and back again count as changes of pitch? After all, the octave leaps do not change the inversion. The answer is the same as in the dimension of phenomenal harmonic rhythm: only identical pitches, not pitch-classes, count as reiterations. The sense of this is plain to the ear. Try playing the passage without the octave shifts; does the harmony have the same sense of movement? Or listen to the beginning of Handel's aria "He was despised" (ex. 4-7), in which he establishes the key of E-flat major simply by sounding the tonic chord for two beats. Would the effect be the same without the leap in the bass? If octave leaps make no difference to the perception of harmony, then such derangements should cause no harmonic effects.

Rests in the bass line, however, pose a more complicated problem. Do they indicate an interruption in the harmonic effect of the bass, thus demanding notation as such, or do bass effects persist through the rests, connecting with the next bass note?

Consider the beginning of Corelli's slow movement once more (ex. 4-5). The quarter rests at the opening affect the sense of meter quite significantly. Because the stability of the bass is missing on those beats, they are easy to perceive as weak beats, so that the gentle duple meter of the opening passage is clear. Later on in measures 5 and 6 a much longer silence is chiefly responsible for one of Corelli's most important harmonic structures, the multilevel progression (see chapter 5). Here, on the higher, more abstract level, the long dominant function of the B-flat major triad persists through the violins' duet until the bass resumes. Then the E-flat harmony acts as a resolution of the dominant and a new beginning at the same time, the familiar harmonic elision typical of so many phrase patterns. On the lower, more immediate level, the violins' duet creates its own syntactic progression. Had the bass continued to sound its B-flat, this progression would have been much less audible, perhaps completely imperceptible. On the other hand, had the bass harmonized the lower-level triads of the violins, Corelli could not have sustained the higher-level long dominant with its musical tension. By remaining silent, the bass engineers a far greater effect than by sounding.

The conclusion offered by Corelli is clear: bass rests deserve notation. The composer can employ the bass voice for powerful effects, one of which is to silence it. However, now consider "The trumpet shall sound" from Handel's *Messiah* (ex. 4-6). Here the rests have an entirely different function, and the clue is that the bass pitch before and after each rest is identical. The rests do not interrupt the immediate effect of the harmonic bass; rather, they are articulations within the harmonic event. The quarter-note eighth-rest figure could be rewritten as a dotted quarter in all parts

Ex. 4-5. Corelli, Concerto op. 6, no. 8, III, mm. 1–6.

Ex. 4-6. Handel, "The trumpet shall sound," no. 48 from *Messiah*, mm. 1–3.

without any damage to the harmonic rhythm. But Handel wishes a crisp, martial fanfare for this aria, and so he writes in the rests to ensure that articulation.

All the foregoing can be summarized in the following rules:

1. If the bass pitch changes after a rest, notate the rest in the graph.
2. If the bass pitch before a rest does not change after it, *and* if one hears an immediate and uninterrupted continuity through the intervening rest, then sum all rests along with all identical pitches surrounding them in one durational symbol.

The bass line at the beginning of "The trumpet shall sound" clearly satisfies both conditions of the second rule, so all the values of the D_2 notes are added together along with the rest. The same applies to the C-sharp$_2$ notes in measure 2. All the instances given of the Corelli concerto satisfy the first rule; in the graph, its bass drops out for the duration of the rest.

The second rule will certainly demand sensitive judgment from time to time. Consider "He was despised," another great Handel aria (ex. 4-7). After a silence of four and one-half beats, Handel's bass reenters on the same B-flat$_2$ that it last sounded in the previous bar (m. 2). The pitch identity clause of rule 2 is satisfied, but can the analyst hear "an immediate and uninterrupted continuity"? There are many factors to consider—the length of the silence, whether there is significant harmonic activity within, whether the link would make harmonic sense—but no magic formula for weighing them, because the immediate context, about which it is impossible to generalize completely, has so much influence on the perception.[5] This graph includes the rests owing to the number of chord changes made

Ex. 4-7. Handel, "He was despised," no. 23 from *Messiah*, mm. 1–4.

by the violins, but others might argue that all those chords have dominant function and so carry the bass pitch through.

In any case, there is no need to mourn the loss of a high-level interpretation, such as the long dominant in the Corelli, in opting for rests, because it is not lost. The more abstract harmonic functions and structures will find their places in other dimensions to come.

One might argue with justice that in certain typical bass-line rhythms—such as the eighth-note/eighth-rest pattern used by composers who want crisp articulation—one hears full quarter notes of bass function even when the pitches change. This may be quite true in many cases, and in fact the stride bass in the Joplin rag (ex. 4-3) produces such a graph because the sustain pedal of the piano can make written eighth notes sound like quarters. Once again, immediate context can bend the rules. In any case, the logic of the first rule still holds. Remember that when interpreting harmonic rhythm, it is not the actual durations that will matter but the rates of change, and the rate of change denoted by successive quarter notes is perceptually equivalent to eighths followed by eighth rests.

WHAT IS THE BASS?

It may be surprising, but the most frequent and most subtle matter of interpretation to be faced while graphing the bass pitch rhythm is the very identity of the bass voice. What qualifies as the bass? It is obvious by now that the easy answer to this—"the lowest sounding pitch"—is the wrong answer, else the Corelli and Handel passages cited earlier would often have the bass among the violins. Any analysis forced to take the lowest available pitch would ignore the composer's power to silence the bass voice for important harmonic effects.

The bass voice is not simply a sound phenomenon but, like any note, also a concept contained in the syntax of certain musical languages. It is a kind of symbol, and the bass voice, like harmony itself, has a number of aspects that contribute to its symbolic presence. One of these is its association with a specific pitch range, often with a specific instrument like the cello or string bass (violone), that identifies it as a special melody with special functions in the texture. The bass is perfectly capable of dropping out of that texture, and that exit and subsequent reentrance can create significant rhythmic articulations for the texture as a whole.

Frederic Chopin certainly considers the bass voice something more than a low pitch. Look at the notation for his first etude of Opus 25 (ex. 4-8). The composer clearly intends some distinction between the A-flat$_2$s in the first measure and those in the second, even though they are identical pitches. While those small-note A-flat$_2$s are sounding, there are phenomenal and finally triadic changes in the harmonies above, but with regard to the bass voice Chopin seems to be saying that there is no "uninterrupted continuity" of the bass A-flat$_2$ through measures 2–5, or else he would have used large notes, as in measure 1. The little notes are a kind of rest in the real bass voice, which Chopin is careful to notate throughout the piece in

Ex. 4-8. Chopin, Etude op. 25, no. 1, mm. 1–8.

the larger notation. Now there is another interruption by a small note in the D-flat$_3$s of measure 5, but since it is so brief and without any accompanying harmonic change, this time it carries through to the next large D-flat$_3$.

So, contrary to expectation, the decision about what will count as the "real" bass voice can be controversial. Analyzing the Bach passage in example 4-9 demands sensitivity to the immediate context as well as familiarity with the baroque musical language. The notation of this ritornello (aria introduction) suggests that the bass comes and goes, as in the Corelli (ex. 4-5). But hearing the piece contradicts that impression. Rather, the viola takes over the role of the bass voice. It leaps as a bass often leaps, that is, among important chord factors, and its timbre is distinct from the solo flute timbre, as in a trio sonata. So the graph of the bass pitch rhythm is continuous, as if there were no rests. But why does Bach risk confusing the issue in a kind of music where the bass and its actions are so essential?

Ex. 4-9. J. S. Bach, "Blute nur," no. 12 from the *St. Matthew Passion*, mm. 1–5.

The reason is in the orchestration of the ritornello. Bach has mimicked a tiny concerto grosso, on Corelli's model, augmenting Corelli's two violin parts with solo flutes. Every concerto grosso must distinguish between the big group (ripieni or tutti) and the small group of soloists (soli), and Bach does so here by contrasting, not the melodic groups themselves but their two basses. He symbolizes the ripieni by a full basso continuo, including organ accompaniment, while articulating the soli group with a kind of miniature bass, represented by the viola, a technique sometimes called "bassetto" (literally, "little bass").[6] Big or little, both low instruments function as a real bass voice.

The concept of the "real bass voice" entails the syntax of traditional functional harmony. There are many musical languages that have no such syntax: music before 1500 and much twentieth-century music. In those kinds of music, the bass voice, if there is a continuous melody that can be perceived as such, has no more harmonic significance than any other melody and contributes nothing distinctive to the dimensional analysis of harmonic rhythm.

CHAPTER 5.

ROOT/QUALITY HARMONIC

RHYTHM

*T*HE DIMENSION of the root/quality rhythm returns to Walter Piston's original insight: harmonic rhythm as the perceived motion caused by changing triads. That insight was both significant and natural since it is the triad that is the locus of the syntax of traditional functional harmony. The root/quality rhythm in dimensional analysis, however, departs from Piston's technique in two important ways.

SYMBOLOGY OF ROOT/QUALITY
RHYTHM

The first departure is the symbology. Compare the analyses of the two Handel passages from *Messiah* briefly discussed in chapter 1 (ex. 1-2; here, ex. 5-1). Both analyses share the same pattern of note duration symbols that quantify the changes. Both explain why one senses faster motion in the second passage than in the first, even though there are many fewer sixteenth notes. But the symbols identifying each triad differ, and they communicate different things.

A Piston analysis uses the traditional Roman numerals to identify each triad. They indicate the chord's root precisely, and more. They identify every chord's relation to a specified key. Furthermore, because we associate certain Roman numerals with certain syntactic functions—I is usually tonic, V and VII are usually dominant, and so on—they carry a lot of information about the triad's role in the syntax of the musical phrase.

Ex. 5-1. Handel, "For unto us," no. 12 from *Messiah*, mm. 20–22, 26–28.

Such information is very important, which is partly why Roman numeral analysis is so widely accepted and used to discuss traditional functional harmony. But the main principle behind dimensional analysis of harmonic rhythm is diffraction, teasing every harmonic feature out from the complicated harmonic phenomenon and graphing it individually, as far as possible. Piston's Roman numeral is too complex a symbol for a root movement analysis, for it summarizes three different harmonic features that are to some extent independent of one another. Triad function and relation to the tonic must wait for their own dimension (chapter 7).

The symbology adopted for the root/quality dimension identifies the triad and that is all. To do so, it must express every triad's two parameters: the pitch of the root and the quality of the triad—that is, major, minor, diminished, augmented.[1] A traditional letter symbol shows the pitch-class of the root. The quality is indicated as follows:

Major triad—upper-case letter
Minor triad—lower-case letter
Diminished triad—lower-case letter followed by $(-)$
Augmented triad—upper-case letter followed by $(+)$

The Handel passages show three of the four types. Inversions are of no concern; the role of the bass in harmonic rhythm is covered in the dimension of bass pitch rhythm (chapter 4).

There is no reason why this symbology cannot be expanded when the situation warrants. Altered triads, such as augmented sixth chords, may require their own distinctive markers. In certain musical languages—impressionism, perhaps—the symbology may have to account for the systematic use of seventh chords or added sixth factors. Traditional music seems not to require the representation of added or subtracted seventh factors in the root/quality dimension (they appear in the phenomenal harmonic rhythm), but if such changes in other kinds of music act syntactically as do triads in functional harmony, the symbology should represent those changes. It may even be necessary to separate root from quality and construct two dimensions of them. In functional harmony these parameters are highly dependent on one another and so require only one graph, but they could conceivably move independently in other harmonic idioms. In short, the symbology can adapt to show the most important changes of the musical language at hand.

Another hearing of Corelli's Adagio (ex. 5-2) shows how this symbology avoids some analytical difficulties. The rhythmic pattern differs only slightly from the bass pitch analysis: it shows the continuity of the C minor triad throughout the second measure while the bass changes to create an illusion of root movement. But the important lesson here is what need not be decided. The passage is transitional, it seems. What key should we declare? Shall we employ secondary dominants or rather denote tiny modulations? All such interpretations are put off for the moment. The only necessities are noting the triad root and its type. The symbology concentrates on the triads' identities and forgets their syntactic function in the music.

Ex. 5-2. Corelli, Concerto op. 6, no. 8, III, mm. 9–14.

HIERARCHICAL ROOT MOVEMENT

The second departure from Piston concerns the introduction of hierarchical analysis, the idea that harmony can move and function on more than one level of structure, more than one perceptual stream at the same time.

Remember that one of the principal difficulties in applying Piston's concept of harmonic rhythm was deciding what counted as a "real" triad, which harmonic events would be assigned a Roman numeral and which would be left with none, mere passing chords (chapter 1). Traditional harmonic theory has habitually distinguished between triads acting strongly in a functional syntax and other triads that are mere coincidences of melodies in a contrapuntal texture. But both history and analysis have shown that it is impossible to define a foolproof way of distinguishing these harmonic phenomena. And this problem is not rare in practice; on the contrary, it is endemic in all but the simplest polyphonic music.

The first measure of Bach's prelude (ex. 5-3) analyzes quite nicely for eight eighth notes before we run into the all too familiar dilemma. What of the B-D dyad in the bass and alto? One view proposes that this chord is a new root change, a motion consistent with the quarter-note eighth-note pattern already established. It is true that either the fifth factor or the root is missing, but so have factors been missing throughout the opening two-voice texture. An opposing view asks the status of the long soprano C-sharp$_5$ (a pedal?) and then points out that the B$_2$ is a classic weak-beat passing tone and the alto D$_4$ a neighbor tone. It is a simpler analysis to hear the B-D motion as a coincidence of contrapuntal motion decorating a sustained A major triad.

The modern view is that both interpretations are correct and both must appear in an analysis.[2] Each view appeals to a different "level" of musical perception, each with its own consistent continuity. The so-called lower level, also called the "surface" level, includes the fastest triad motions that make a sensible progression. In Bach's prelude, this level would comprise the quarter- and eighth-note durations. The "higher" level—slower, often more abstract, yet sensible through its musical effects—is the more contrapuntal view and subsumes many of those short-lived triads under a single dotted whole note (in mm. 1–2). In the higher-level view, there is basically one triad sounding in each measure; other chords are merely coincidences of melodic motion.

Analyzing more than one level of root/quality rhythm not only solves dilemmas like this one but sometimes leads to unsuspected insights into a musical passage. But a single prickly moment does not always mean the presence of more than one level of root progression. How does one justify a multilevel analysis?

There are no ironclad rules, but the first and foremost consideration is perceptibility of the different levels. Hear how carefully Bach insists on the audibility of the first level of root/quality change in the opening of his prelude. Two voices only, but the strong harmonic identities are absolutely clear. There is nothing to suggest that any tone is not a fully functioning triad factor until the seventh beat, when the soprano begins to acquire a pedal quality and some pitches in the lower voices function more ambivalently. But by then, even as the higher level becomes substantial, it is much too late to question the integrity of the first. That is why Bach can compose the second measure in a much different way, the octave leaps in the bass nearly melding the first level with the second, only to break free again in the third measure.

The more abstract level has its own justification. Every bass note, save that B on the weak ninth beat, is a factor of the A major triad, as are all beats in the soprano, save two, and half the beats in the alto. Similarly, all the sustained pitches in the second measure are factors of an E dominant

Ex. 5-3. J. S. Bach, Prelude in A from *The Well-Tempered Clavier*, vol. 2, mm. 1–6.

seventh. With Bach's smooth voice-leading giving all the other notes status as nonharmonic tones, it is quite easy to hear the "big" harmonies in the first two measures.

A second consideration is the continuity of the progression. Do the imagined triads link up, or are they disparate, fleeting instants? The first level nearly disappears in Bach's second measure, because the E major triad sustains nearly as long as it does on the second level; however, the first level does connect functionally with its characteristic faster motion in the third measure. Handel's figured bass, on the other hand, rules out the likelihood of a very fleet, microprogression (ex. 5-1), simply because he asks the organist handling the continuo part to sustain each chord for a full quarter note. Continuity also implies consistency in the duration pattern itself. Part of the reason that the second-level Bach analysis makes sense is its easy acceleration from four-beat durations (dotted-quarter beats), to three, to two, and finally to one.

A third consideration of multilevel analysis is the kind of voice-leading in the texture. Disjunct melodic motion—leaps, as in Bach's bass voice at the beginning of the prelude—suggest real root motion since, if the function and identity of the triad were not that important, Bach would use the preferred conjunct motion. Smooth voice-leading, however, never disqualifies a level of progression automatically. See how in measures 4–5 step-motion predominates, even in the bass, yet there is a new triad on every eighth-note beat. This is one of the miracles of Bach's art: without compromising the highest ideals of melodic writing he can yet make every note count for harmonic effect.

Finally, the order of the triads in any progression must make sense. More technically, the functions of the chords must make a proper syntax. The second-level progression at the beginning is as strong and clear as could be: tonic, dominant, and then tonic again in the third measure. But so is the much faster first-level progression. There is a similar alternation of tonic and dominant until a flurry of subdominant-functioning triads leads very appropriately into the longer dominant, reminiscent of a half cadence. Even the rapid-fire changes in measures 4 and 5 make sense, although many functions are weak or ambiguous. Undirected, random-like triads are not to be found here. This is yet another feature of Bach's superb control of counterpoint, since, from the contrapuntal point of view, triads are nothing but phenomena produced by simultaneously sounding melodies.

Considering the functions of the triads might appear to be getting ahead of ourselves. After all, I have not yet graphed the rhythm of harmonic function (chapter 7). But this is not a cart-before-horse matter or a question of circular logic. A great many human perceptions feed back on one another. In this case, triad function and triad identity, even existence, inform one another in a kind of circular perception.[3]

Before moving on to more complex instances of root/quality rhythm, consider the textural rhythm of the prelude in the light of the bilevel triad motions: there is never a moment when an eighth-note duration is not sounded somewhere in the texture. It is one of the more delightful paradoxes of musical experience that a piece can have an utterly consistent, relentless pulse like this yet give the same impressions of rest and motion, pause and acceleration, tension and resolve that freer rhythms might give. The dimension graphed on two levels begins to reveal how this paradox can work.

GRAPHING AMBIGUOUS TRIADS

Identifying the triads in the prelude, even on the more abstract second level, does not require much interpretation. Bach's deployment of the three voices is so economical that most of the time all the factors of the triad sound, and there is no doubt of the root. Even at the beginning, with only two voices, the harmonic functions and bass pitches make the interpretations easy. But in other passages triads may be incompletely sketched or barely implied. The analyst must then interpret the changes with imagination and sensitivity to the musical language of the composition, as in example 5-4, from Bach's *Mass in B Minor*.

This ritornello is for flute and continuo only, and Bach left no figured bass, so any "hard data" for analysis must come from the two voices.[4] With such a barebones texture, simple questions such as "When do we hear the first triad change?" are not so simple. The chord on the downbeat of the first measure is not a triad. To graph a rest at that point is nonsense because it would signal some kind of disruption in the continuity of the progression, a disruption that no Bach lover would hear.[5] But the two pitches, in isolation, have equal priority as roots. Neither one is outweighed by the other, as it might be if another factor were present.

But of course, they are not in isolation but in a context leaving little doubt that the C-sharp$_6$ is the triad factor. First, the C-sharp$_6$ is not prepared during the previous beat, whereas the B$_3$ in the bass sustains, as in a suspension. Second, the flute leaps away, down to E$_5$. Baroque melodies rarely leap except among chord factors. Third, a change of chord is expected on a strong beat of the measure. Fourth, the change of triad from B minor to A-sharp diminished is immediately confirmed, so quickly that the perceiving mind can retrospectively hear the past and revise or confirm its best guesses.[6]

Why graph the change before that confirmation rather than with it? One reason is that there would be nothing else to write there, leaving a gap in the continuity. A better reason is that, even more than a single note or the

Ex. 5-4. J. S. Bach, Benedictus, from the *Mass in B Minor*, mm. 1–12.

Ex. 5-4. *Continued*

bass voice, a triad is a concept, not simply a physical phenomenon of sounding tones. Those tones elicit the concept in perceiving listeners who know the musical language, and all the tones are seldom required. Some contexts are so well defined that a single tone can cause the listener to hear a triad change and identify the new chord; this is one of them. The graph must show, in the analyst's best judgment, when the new triad is perceived. Most times, this judgment is intuitive and automatic, based on experience of the musical language. Technical reasons like those already cited can justify a decision, but the decision itself is rarely a matter of such calculation.

The more abstract the level, the more analytical experience counts and, often, the more challenges to an interpretation one can expect. It may seem odd that a single F-sharp major triad represents the entire third measure in the second root/quality graph. After all, there are but two F-sharps in the whole bar—with none in the bass—lasting for a grand total of half a beat. But this is to miss Bach's magic tricks with pitches. What does that relatively long E-sharp$_4$ in the flute imply? Obviously, it is a temporary leading tone to F-sharp$_4$, whose resolution is delayed and then decorated. That F-sharp$_4$ resolving the leading tone, in another composer's hand, could have lasted two long beats. And the context of the third measure? It follows directly on a measure in which the long B minor triad, on the second level, is quite unmistakable: all but four notes are factors of that chord. So Bach can afford to take chances with ornamentation, for dominant harmony is what listeners familiar with his musical language are expecting.

In the eighth measure Bach withdraws the bass and allows the flute to soar alone with a melody that is the picture of smooth step-motion. Without melodic arpeggiation and without a bass voice, it might appear that the harmonic progression must stop; there is nothing to analyze. Actually, it is quite easy to hear, and analyze, a most sensible progression because Bach has already established the rules of interpreting these flute triplets. In measures 5–8, with the continuo helping to define each triad, it becomes clear that the first and third notes of each triplet group are triad factors. That strategy, having been practiced for three measures, continues with ease in measure 8, even without the bass, whose absence, by the way, makes it all the more apparent that the solo is an elaboration of a B major triad. That is why the last eighth note of the first-level graph is described with a capital *B*; the D-sharp is still perceived, although no longer heard, at that moment.

Harmonic rhythm recognizes the expectations that are part of the listening experience, even when, on occasion, those expectations are surprised. When the bass reaches the D-natural$_3$ in measure 9, it is a mistake to read the flute's triplet all at once and record "D+"; the most recent progressions have been governed by the key of E minor, and no A-sharp is on the horizon. Instead, the analyst graphs "D" until that moment when the A-sharp$_5$ unexpectedly converts the major into an augmented triad and moves the tonality back to B minor. In a larger sense, of course, such a modulation was indeed expected eventually, but the first-level root/quality graph describes only the most local, moment-to-moment perceptions.

HARMONIC CONVERGENCE AND
OTHER CONSIDERATIONS

There are a few more general considerations regarding the hierarchical graphing of root/quality rhythm. A quick survey of another ritornello, the Domine Deus from Bach's *Mass in B Minor* (ex. 5-5), raises two of them immediately.

The first outstanding feature of this graph is that there is a third level of root movement. One should always be cautious about making the graph unnecessarily complex, and rhythmic levels should be introduced with very good reason. The more abstract the level, the more caution is required. In this case, however, the case for a third one is quite convincing. Bach's counterpoint, so simple and innocent to the ear, provides for three rhythmic streams with remarkable consistency.

The first level, dominated by eighth-note motion, is unquestionable. Bach's own figured bass ratifies it. The second level becomes real as soon as the bass breaks into a compound melody at the end of the first measure, linking the G major triad with the previous step-motion and articulating a clear change with the D major triad. Besides that, consider the long C$_5$ in the flute in measure 2. It sounds and acts like an appoggiatura, but if the only harmonic rhythm available moves in eighth-notes, then it is a most ungrammatical appoggiatura because it resolves much too late, after the chords have twice changed. In fact, the C actually becomes a chord factor again on the second eighth before it resolves. As a young man, Bach was criticized for incorporating strange dissonances into his music, and this would indeed be most strange were it not for the slower stream of harmonic rhythm, against which this appoggiatura resolves quite normally within the chord and in plenty of time. What Bach's critics lacked was the experience required to discern the second level along with the first. By measure 9, this idea of constructing two levels of dissonance is so persuasive that he dares to use two different durations at once. The strings play an appoggiatura chord that resolves within the fast stream while the flute has the longer version that only makes sense in the slower stream. By the rules of counterpoint it looks as though Bach has written an unconscionable dissonance for the flute, for it grates against the A in the bass and then against the entire chord in the strings before resolving. But within his own

Ex. 5-5. J. S. Bach, Domine Deus, from the *Mass in B Minor*, mm. 1–16.

rules of multilevel harmonic rhythm it is completely grammatical and has an inimitable bittersweetness that only grows more intense as the passage continues.

The most abstract third level is the most difficult to hear, as it should be. It reflects, first of all, Bach's unusual reiteration of the opening flute motive, three times in all without essential change. There is a lot of harmonic activity, but on the larger scale the music has gone nowhere by the

Ex. 5-5. *Continued*

end of measure 3. Notice that within these measures there are no root position triads lasting even as long as an eighth note, except G triads. Considered as a compound melody, the bass line moves only by step, suggesting melodic elaboration of the tonic, not strong harmonic functions. Then two musical events confirm the abstraction after the fact. The bass drops out in measure 4 when the key begins to change. Thus it seems sure

Ex. 5-5. *Continued*

that the bass voice symbolized a big, stable harmony; if not, why not participate in the modulation? It returns only to set up an even longer dominant pedal on A, again confirming its rather constrained role of identifying long, abstract triads. This time it is unmistakable; the bass does nothing but sound dominant harmony for eight measures.

One could argue with some justice that the listener is not immediately aware of the second and third levels and it is premature to graph them starting in measure 1. This is reasonable, and a variant graph might delay their onset for a measure, or even two, in the case of the third level.[7] This point speaks to the second consideration of multilevel graphing: the number of levels is not permanent, even for a short passage. Just because a rhythmic stream begins does not mean it must live forever. The Domine Deus shows at least two places where graphs simply cease: the third level in measures 4 and 5 and the first level at the end.

In the first case, the abstract third level simply drops out because the bass ceases to support it and too many contradictory pitches in the upper voices undermine its integrity. It resumes when that support returns in measure 6. In the second case, the first-level rhythm does not really stop but slows so much that it coincides with second-level motion in measure 12. I call such coincidence "convergence" and will show in part II that this affects the musical dynamic significantly. Bach alters his counterpoint among the flute, strings, and bass so subtly that the eighth-note stream of root rhythm dissolves away with absolutely no loss of speed in the melodies of the texture. The continuity is impeccable.

When the convergence lasts so long, it makes little sense to continue the upper graph when it will merely copy a lower one. There is nothing sacrosanct about the upper such that it must continue. On the other hand, the sudden convergence in measure 7 stands written out because the three streams very soon diverge again.

Generally speaking, the more abstract graphs are not only slower but simpler. The harmonies heard more abstractly are unambiguous indicators of the prevailing key and have strong functions. This is why the third level disappears in measures 4 and 5; the modulation dislocates for a moment the tonal center and prevents any long-held triad from taking hold. Rhythmic patterns are also simpler, particularly with regard to the metric structure. The first-level root rhythm of the Domine Deus shows a good deal of offbeat syncopation at the quarter-note level (mm. 8–12). The second level simplifies the syncopation to the half-note level or removes the offbeat effect entirely (m. 8). This gravitation to the strong beat and the preference for strong harmonic functions in the abstract upper levels responds to the cognitive need for coherent organization, or structure, in perception. As individual events grow more abstract, less explicitly defined, and further apart in the time stream, stronger relations between them are required to maintain the patterns that listeners have learned to recognize from their musical experience. Strong harmonic functions and simple, strong-beat metric patterns are just such patterns.

Photographing or sketching a complex building such as Chartres Cathedral produces analogous results. Up close, we capture all manner of detail, regular and irregular. To photograph the entire west facade, however, means retreating to a point where we might no longer see that each semi-

Chartres cathedral. Photograph by Étienne Houvet.

circular sculpture (tympanum) over the doors has a different program; we only see that they are semicircular because semi-circles are explicit, regular, and familiar patterns. Further back, the picture might include the whole church, with two towers flanking the building to the north and south. We don't notice that they are mismatched.

Fortunately, in the multilevel root graphs and in other kinds of music theory, the detail can be seen alongside the big picture, and that comparison can show certain things about the passage that otherwise would be difficult to understand. Already the technique has explained the musical syntax behind Bach's strange dissonances. The harmonic rhythm runs on more than one level of motion, which means that his counterpoint does too. If that were not true, every downbeat from measure 9 through 12 would constitute a gross violation of the rules of counterpoint and therefore should sound perfectly awful, instead of marvelously wonderful.

Although example 5-5 does not show the other dimensions of harmonic rhythm, the hierarchical graph of the root movement begins to hint at the reasons for this ritornello's dynamic shape. First, look back at the score for a reminder that the passage develops perhaps just two motives and moves with consummate continuity, powered by constant eighths and sixteenths throughout. There are no grand pauses, no obvious changes. But consistency never means monotony in Bach's counterpoint; there is a moment of comparative relaxation, a climax, and a resolution. We don't need the graph to tell us that or to find the places, but the graph helps to explain why they can occur without disturbing the effortless flow of this music.

The first moment that leaps to the eye is measure 7, where, suddenly, all three levels agree for the first time. The opening six measures, quite complex, have worked hard to present the key motives and most of all to firmly establish in the ear the cognitive reality of the three levels of harmonic rhythm. When they coincide, the music seems suddenly spacious and relaxed but without the least letup of melodic activity.

Soon the streams diverge again, almost violently, since the audible cues for the faster motion are Bach's strange appoggiaturas. The three streams of measures 9–12 are like the beginning, except that the first and second levels are both syncopated, each in its own way. Here the metric tension is highest; this is the climax of the ritornello.

Then, when the bass finally breaks free of its pedal, its increased speed brings the third level nearly into line with the second. The first has already melted into the second in measure 12, and as the ritornello relaxes into its final cadence, all the syncopations disappear.

Hierarchical analysis of root harmonic rhythm is necessary because it often avoids the frequent conflict between a strictly triadic and a contrapuntal interpretation of harmonic phenomena, and it is fruitful because the comparison of such diverse streams can explain musical effects that might be difficult to deduce from the score alone. In that sense it is a small-scale version of the dimensional technique as a whole. There is no reason to think that Walter Piston would disapprove of such hierarchical pictures. They are logical extensions of his original insight.

CHAPTER 6.

DENSITIES OF HARMONIC

RHYTHM

*O*BVIOUSLY A TRIAD can progress to another with quiescent subtlety, with terrific force, and with every degree of emphasis in between. Debussy begins his Prelude no. 1, book 1, "Danseuses de Delphes," (ex. 6-1) with a series of six-note chords, but after the first it becomes clear that only four real melodies are in counterpoint; the parallel octaves in right and left hands are amplifications of the outermost voices. For one beat in the third measure these outer voices alone continue the motion; then the alto joins in. In the fourth measure we hear seven-note chords for the first time and as many as five active voices.

The density graph just below the first-level root/quality graph in example 6-1 charts these differences. The number of staff lines touched by the vertical bar indicates the number of voices that have moved to articulate a new triad. In the first chord of the piece, all sound for the first time; they have "moved" out of silence—appeared, so to speak—and so the density of the B-flat major triad is six. The A diminished triad has a much lower density (three), owing to the loss of two independent voices and because the B-natural₃ in the alto is not a chord factor, so that, although a new pitch, it does not help to define the second triad. But all four voices contribute to the third triad, the unusual F augmented; the density rises to four.

The root harmonic rhythm continues with unabated quarter notes in the next two bars, but the emphasis on those changes is less. The articulation of the B diminished triad is accomplished by the bass alone; the other voices are either motionless (alto, tenors 1 and 2) or dissonant (soprano).[1] Its density is therefore 1, the lowest possible. Density rises again when the alto moves in parallel thirds with the bass and the soprano G_4 becomes a triad factor, and then more dramatically with the seven-note chords, but no change achieves a density of seven because the parallel octaves are considered to be single voices. The progression leading up to the cadence on F, however, presents a peak of contrapuntal density not heard since the phrase's beginning.

Density, then, is this degree of emphasis on a harmonic change. The graph in example 6-1 measures this salience by observing Debussy's coun-

Ex. 6-1. Debussy, Prelude no. 1, book 1, "Danseuses de Delphes," mm. 1–10.

Ex. 6-1. *Continued*

terpoint, how he moves the various independent melodies in the texture, but that is only one of many possible ways of measuring density. In an orchestral work it may be more profitable to count the number of instruments that change a chord. In a composition without triads, counting pitch-classes, or even all the notes, may be best. But whatever the criterion chosen, density is an explicitly dependent variable, the only dimension in dimensional analysis that makes no sense by itself. It must derive from another dimension and be "density of . . ." some aspect of harmony. In example 6-1 the graph shows the density of the first-level root rhythm in Debussy's prelude, with counterpoint supplying the discrete "units" of measurement.

The density of a single chord means little. But when densities change from one chord to another, those changes can affect the overall picture of harmonic rhythm in two important ways.

First, density affects the perception—and therefore the analysis—of higher levels of harmonic rhythm. Debussy's prelude presents a single stream of triad motion until the third bar, when a second, more abstract level develops. The density graph helps to justify this analysis. The first six chords are of similar emphasis; none sounds like an ornament of another. But the second beat of measure 3 is barely articulated by the bass. This allows that measure's downbeat chord, the B-flat triad that also represents the stability of the tonal center, to anchor the smooth voice-leading that proceeds from it. Similarly, the relatively weak density of the A-flat triad in measure 2 of Corelli's Adagio (see ex. 6-2, m. 2) partly accounts for its subsumption into the C minor chord on the second level. Density rarely decides such analyses by itself, but because, by definition, it describes the emphasis on a new chord, it logically contributes to them.

Second, changes in density can in and of themselves create patterns. Because such patterns become apparent in the time-stream of the music, they are rhythms, distinct from the root rhythms from which they may derive.

The second phrase of Debussy's prelude (ex. 6-1, mm. 6–10), for instance, recapitulates the harmonic progression and root rhythm of the first phrase. But the composer doubles the textural rhythm by displacing the greater part of each chord to the offbeat. The strong part of each beat is left to the chromatic alto melody and bass, which, despite all the missing factors, succeed in articulating the progression we heard less than half a minute before. The offbeat chords merely confirm the inferences that first come to mind. But now the onset of each triad is understated, and the density graph is a minimalist version of the first two measures. It is as if the volume control on harmonic rhythm has been suddenly turned down, distinguishing the two matched phrases dynamically. Debussy's procedure here is a microcosm of the strategy of the whole piece, perhaps even of much of his musical language. The second phrase denatures the harmonic content of the first, requiring the listener to work harder at inferring the key elements of syntax to make sense of the music's direction, and it is that effort, combined with the speedier textural rhythm, that makes the second phrase more motile and less stable.

DENSITY OF WHAT?

If density is a kind of volume control on harmonic rhythm, the choice of what constitutes it, the criterion for analysis, is critical.

Harmonic density has two quantities: amount and duration. But the duration is identical to the dimension from which it derives; in the Debussy example the duration of each density bar is the same as the note for the root graph above it. Standard musical notation would duplicate the information already there. But the amount of density describes the emphasis on a particular change in harmonic aspect. This is new information.

In theory, any dimension has density, a varying degree of emphasis on its individual events. The bass pitch dimension, however, is too elementary to have density that can be measured; the only degree of emphasis in a bass pitch is dynamic emphasis, a sforzando attack or subito piano, but that leads to insoluble problems of measuring continuous phenomena. How would one compare an *sf* in the bass to a *ff* or an *fp*? In practice, only the dimensions made of plural, discrete elements can be discretely graphed. For textural rhythm, one could count the number of notes or instruments or singers making each onset; for phenomenal harmonic rhythm, the number of new notes in the chord; for function, perhaps the number of voices responsible for creating the new function. I do not know whether the analytical results obtained with these kinds of densities would be of any use, but they remain theoretical possibilities. The choice of criterion and the choice of the precise unit of density depends greatly on the musical language in question.[2]

With musical languages of traditional harmonic function, I analyze the density of root/quality rhythm by observing the counterpoint that creates the triad changes, as in the Debussy prelude (ex. 6-1). Simply put, the greater the number of voices that change pitches when articulating a new triad, the higher the density.[3] This criterion for density appeals to a long tradition in Western music, the concept of harmony as a happy coincidence of independent melodies, and is particularly apt for a great body of music, from Renaissance motets to baroque keyboard works to classical quartets, that restricts itself to a fairly constant performance medium and often a constant number of voices. Without significant range in dynamics or orchestration, pieces like these depend on counterpoint for dynamic contrasts.

Dissonances such as suspensions or the chromatic alto in the Debussy prelude do not contribute to the density of a new triad because they are not factors. This may seem counterintuitive to some, for, after all, dissonances attract attention, do they not?

The issue turns on the precise density we want to analyze. If one were to graph the density of phenomenal harmonic rhythm (chapter 3), then dissonance could certainly count for "extra points" in the amounts registered because there is no question that dissonance in many musical languages draws attention to changes of chord. In certain contexts, one might well want to make such a graph.

But if the density derives from the root/quality graph, it must reflect the emphasis on changes in just those aspects. When one is in doubt about the identity of a root, confidence about its changing declines, in most instances. Any dissonance necessarily makes the identity of the chord less explicit, since it represents the possibility of another root interpretation with itself being a triad member. Looking ahead to the Corelli Adagio (ex. 6-2), there is a suspension in the violins on the fourth beat of measure 2, a typically baroque way to emphasize an oncoming cadence. But which tone is the suspension and which the triad factor? The E-flat$_4$/F$_4$ combination creates the possibility that the "real" triad is E-flat major, not B-flat major, that the F$_4$ will resolve up. That would mean no root change from the previous eighth note.[4] The dissonance is indeed memorable but not in its triadic aspect, for it clouds the salience of the root movement by making it less certain that the root has really changed on that fourth beat. In fact, it is easy to prove that any dissonant combination of tones provides at least one other interpretation of the root.[5] So in the root dimension, obscurity of identity takes away from what acoustic harshness would emphasize in the phenomenal dimension.

Once the criterion for measuring density is settled, there is the matter of notation, how to express this amount of emphasis. Simple numerals that describe the number of active voices is one possibility of course, but the bar-type graph used in the examples has one significant advantage: it shows the trends and large-scale patterns at a glance. Rarely does a single change in density, even when dramatically higher or lower, make much difference to the overall interpretation. As shown in the Debussy, it is the larger periods of high-density or low-density changes that articulate harmonic rhythm peculiar to this dimension.

WHAT IS A VOICE?

The only significant interpretation for the analyst of contrapuntal density is: what counts as a voice? In the analysis of the Debussy prelude (ex. 6-1), the opening parallel octaves in the left hand and later on in the right hand counted as a single contrapuntal voice. Why? Simply because such voice-leading is traditionally prohibited in counterpoint. When composers write parallel octaves at length, as in a great deal of piano music, they do not intend two contrapuntal voices, but rather a single, amplified voice. It is a means of changing the color of a melody.

The Corelli Adagio (ex. 6-2) changes its texture quite frequently from the larger tutti ensemble down to the soli. Such changes make it more difficult to decide how many voices are in play. At the beginning the solo cello parallels the bass; the two lines count as a single voice, until the end of bar 2 when they become independent. Why is the density of the second triad (B-flat major) six, not four? Because the viola has moved up to the F_4 and the second violin down to it; although the two instruments double the note, they have moved to it independently and thus maintain their integrity as independent voices. We count the F_4 twice. Meanwhile the solo second violin enters the texture for the first time. That instantiates a new contra-puntal voice. Again the two soloists share the F4 briefly, but each moves off independently. That F_4 also counts as two.

Generally, voices arriving at a common pitch count as independent voices and maintain their independence afterward unless they continue to double one another. Consider the third beat in measure 2 (ex. 6-2). At this point, Corelli has the tutti violins play the same melodies as the soli. The tutti violins have been independent up to that third beat and so count

Ex. 6-2. Corelli, Concerto op. 6, no. 8, "Christmas," III, mm. 1–17.

individually on that beat (density is 6) but thereafter merely double the soloists and lose their independence. That is why the density declines severely from then on.

The Allegro section brings up once more the matter of the compound melody (see chapter 3) The first violins play one note at a time, but so fast that they create the perception of two melodies. Since the present criterion

Ex. 6-2. *Continued*

for density is the number of voices, each perceived voice counts, even though they do not arrive precisely coincident with the new triad.

In baroque music the figured bass represents an unknowable variable in the calculation of density. In the Corelli piece, the probability that a keyboard player could invent a seventh, truly independent melody is low, but

Allegro

in sonatas for one soprano instrument and continuo, such an expectation would not be unreasonable in the eighteenth century. But since every realization would be different, with considerable inconsistencies, there is no verifiable way of including the figured bass in the density dimension. Improvisatory elements remain beyond the purvey of analytical methods that are based on the score.

All this assumes my own density criterion for traditional root progressions: the number of active contrapuntal voices that articulate a new triad. Other criteria for measuring the emphasis on root changes are possible, and densities of other dimensions are certainly possible and often desirable and they will demand their own criteria. The examples here represent more of an illustration of the kinds of issues to be considered and less of a prescription of how to apply a specific technique.

In conclusion, it is well to remember that, of all dimensions of harmonic rhythm, density says the least by itself and profits the most from comparison with the others. It explicitly depends on at least one other dimension. Furthermore, even within that context density is by no means a free variable. That is why it is all too easy to read too much meaning into local density fluctuations. Root changes by the interval of a second (e.g., C major to D minor) obviously have a higher probability of high density because there are no common tones. Still, dissonant counterpoint can always reduce density, and there are plenty of places where more voices move than would be absolutely necessary to effect the new root, which, after all, the composer chooses. The endings of Bach fugues come to mind, where the composer often abandons a smoother texture of sustained tones for a climax of dense harmonic rhythm.

A similar example from the Allegro section of the Corelli movement also comes to mind (ex. 6-2). Notice that in measures 11–13 the downbeat chords are very dense compared to the upbeats. Ordinarily this might be expected to produce a rather heavy-handed duple meter, but here the effect is nearly reversed because the downbeat chords have dominant function with respect to the upbeats. This is a metric displacement of the normal downbeat-tonic, upbeat-dominant association, and the density disparity amplifies this syncopated effect (see chapter 8). Then the disparity suddenly evaporates. In measure 14 Corelli reconfigures the first violin part so that, instead of representing two additional melodies, it doubles the second violin and viola, essentially disappearing into the counterpoint. The effect? While the dominant-tonic relations in measures 10–13 actually change the sense of key, the same relations in measures 14–16 exist within the superior key of E-flat major, as secondary dominants. These relations, with significant rhythmic effects, show up in the functional dimension still to come.

CHAPTER 7.

RHYTHM OF HARMONIC

FUNCTIONS

*W*HEN A FOLKSINGER strums a guitar accompaniment, voice-leading rarely comes into play, not even unconsciously. The chords are virtually pure harmonic structures; one cannot speak of inner melodic voices, often not even of a bass. Yet the progression harmonizing the vocal melody makes sense in a way that goes beyond simply being consonant with it. The chords themselves have a coherence, an order whose justification is independent of the singer's melody and certainly independent of the voice-leading conventions associated with contrapuntal harmonic languages. This order, this purely harmonic syntax, is, of course, the hallmark of the so-called common practice period of Western art music.[1] The elements of that syntax are harmonic functions.

The rhythmic importance of harmonic functions is hard to overstate, for functions create much of the dynamic we experience in harmonic motion, the interplay between stability and instability, moments when musical tension is created and then resolved. All the emphasis on the interdependence of harmony and counterpoint through the centuries, and in the foregoing chapters, is well and good, but function is harmony's emancipation from counterpoint. The strumming of the folksinger shows that when functions are clear and strong, melodic integrity of inner parts can be dispensed with. Harmonic progression, and its rhythm, compensate.

Such a dispensation is hardly desirable for itself. Emancipation from constraints in the arts is not always a good thing, as Stravinsky once proclaimed, even though artistic "revolutions" attract a lot of attention.[2] When harmonic functions began to change the language of secular music in the sixteenth century, melodic integrity of the several parts—our voice-leading grammar—was never abandoned. True, certain aspects began to relax, as when instrumental writing and then vocal writing took advantage of new harmonic organizations to leap among chord factors even when they were dissonant, a melodic freedom previously denied them.[3] Rather, art music of the "common practice" added harmonic functions, as another powerful means of articulation and organization, to a language already rich with them, without giving up very much in the aesthetics of good part writing. The reconciliation of these two ideals in composition lies at the heart of the great achievements of the next three centuries.

The sense of order of harmonic function is born of the relations deriving from the triad's position in a key as they are understood by the musical community equipped to perceive them.[4] That is probably why Walter Piston, who first defined harmonic rhythm, used Roman numeral symbols to mark harmonic changes. Such symbols communicate nothing about the duration of a harmony but much about the triad's relation to the governing key and thus about its harmonic function. When properly deployed, distinct harmonic functions create musical phrases by articulating beginning, middle, and cadence, as has long been known. On the high level of structure, harmony contributes mightily to phrase rhythms and on occasion creates modulation rhythms. Within the phrase, there is the rhythm of the functions themselves as they change from one to another.

The dimension of functional harmonic rhythm adopts the three functions of tonic, dominant, and subdominant traditionally recognized in triadic analysis and articulated by Hugo Riemann in the nineteenth century.[5] The tonic function connotes the harmonic stability that grounds a phrase at its beginning and resolves with minimum tension at its end. The dominant is its opposite pole. It conveys maximum instability through the presence of the leading tone of the key, which epitomizes and drives the dominant's tendency toward the tonic. The subdominant, the least clearly defined function of the three, mediates between the tonic and dominant.[6]

Thus the complete functional syntax of tonic-subdominant-dominant-tonic defines a stable harmonic structure. This pattern, of course, is no law of nature but simply a grammatical convention that, like all grammatical conventions, is capable of coherent transformation, responding to the particular context at hand. Half cadences, interrupted phrases, even simple oscillations of tonic and dominant can suffice as structural articulation over short periods, but there is nothing quite so satisfying or conclusive as the complete syntax. In their explicitly linguistic *Generative Theory of Tonal Music*, Fred Lerdahl and Ray Jackendoff built it right into the rules for a well-formed grammar.[7]

GRAPHING

Alessandro Scarlatti's two-voice ritornello from one of his opere serie (ex. 7-1) serves to can introduce the basics of graphing the dimension of harmonic function. Since there are only three functions, we need only three symbols: I, IV, and V.[8] The strong correlation with the root rhythm is both obvious and logical, but it is far from perfect. The functional rhythm of the second measure, for instance, is more sedate than the root rhythm because all three triads share the same dominant function (V). Nor is it ever safe to make an automatic translation from the traditional Roman numeral to its most probable function (e.g., ii is always subdominant). Context affects harmonic function perhaps more than any other dimension, and sensitive judgment is indispensable. There are two G minor triads that even within the governing key of G minor have dominant function because they participate in the I 6/4–V cadential formula (mm. 7, 9).

The function graph must declare the key in force, since to speak of traditional harmonic functions without reference to a key means nothing. When the music modulates, the new referent must be indicated (see mm. 3–5). If a triad mediates the modulation by acting as a pivot chord, a traditional double analysis should indicate this, as in measure 3. The double analysis does not, strictly speaking, differentiate a local rhythmic event, but it may affect the ultimate interpretation of a completed graph. A double analysis always implies a kind of retrospective listening, a reinterpretation of a harmonic event already past. When the pivot chord lasts so long that the listener is unlikely to be able to remember its attack point, the new interpretation may be bracketed. Or we might bracket an alternative attack point that is closer to the definitive change of key, such as the last bass note in measure 5, to show where the listener might focus the reinterpretation. Such improvisations should reflect the act of listening as closely as possible.

If a new triad wrenches the tonal center from one place to another without mediation, as in measure 4, the new tonal center symbol (here, "c") appears before the first chord that can be perceived to function in the new key. Writing the symbols above or below the notes does not affect interpretation but makes the analysis of quickly modulating passages easier to read.

There are no rests in functional rhythm; the graph is continuous.

FUNCTIONAL EMBEDDING

Scarlatti's ritornello contains unusually simple functional rhythms because their progression plays out on a single level of structure. The graph is but

Ex. 7-1. Scarlatti, "Di' ch'è l'ombra," from *La Principessa*, mm. 1–10.

one stream, one line of symbols. This is rare. Even more than root movements, harmonic functions are subject to hierarchical organization: a progression of two or more functions can be embedded in a single function that participates on its own level in a perceptually separate progression.

Embedding occurs in all human languages; analogies with harmonic embedding are easy to find.

He knows he doesn't understand what is going on.

No one would have any trouble understanding this sentence, and yet it includes three levels of grammatical function. The "main" level consists of a subject (noun), a verb, and their object:

He (subject) knows (verb) [he doesn't understand what is going on.] (object)

But the answer to "He knows what?" yields an object that is itself a complete syntax of subject, verb, and object:

He (subject) doesn't understand (verb) [what is going on.] (object)

And once again the object of "He doesn't understand" makes its own complete sentence:

What (subject) is going on? (verb)

Words that we think of as verbs can participate, on a higher level, in constructions that normally function as nouns. Harmonic functions of one sort can, analogously, build a higher-level harmonic function of a completely different, even opposite sort.

As with the hierarchical relations among root movement (chapter 5), it is impossible to write a comprehensive set of rules applying to all circumstances of functional embedding because the immediate context, whose details cannot be generalized, often plays a decisive role. But certain harmonic techniques that by their very nature involve embedding—voice-leading, sequence patterns, pedal points, deceptive cadences, secondary dominants—can offer exemplars for analysis.

The details of Corelli's counterpoint in his Adagio movement cause some passages to have more functional complexity than others that sound very similar. The Allegro section, for instance, has a number of dominant function triads foreign to the principal key of E-flat major. In the first four bars (ex. 7-2, mm. 9-12) they are graphed as brief modulations to C minor, G minor, and F minor, each key displacing the previous one in the percep-

Ex. 7-2. Corelli, Concerto op. 6, no. 8, III, mm. 9–17.

Ex. 7-2. *Continued*

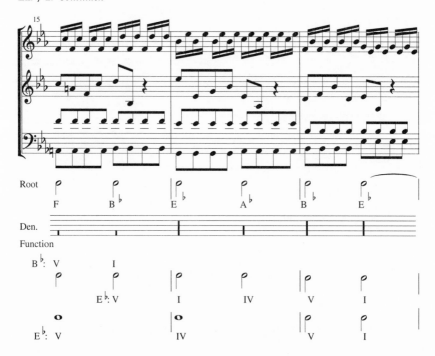

tion of functional relations, as happened in the Scarlatti ritornello. Thereafter, however, the same kind of writing yields secondary dominant interpretations and embedded functions. Why so?

One difference is in the voice-leading of the bass. In the first measures the bass leaps to new leading tones, emphasizing their harmonic function of defining new tonics. After measure 13, however, new leading tones arise from smooth, conjunct motion, which suggests more melodic function, less harmonic. This makes it easier to perceive the progressions as melodic elaborations of a higher-level functions, just as passing chords made of coincidental passing and neighbor tones are so perceived.

Another difference is in the density of the chord changes (see chapter 6). Corelli announces the arrival of each new key by making each new dominant very dense compared to its surroundings (mm. 11, 12, 13). But again, after measure 13 all borrowed dominants are low-density chords, which maximizes their melodic aspect at the expense of their harmonic.

Why then the embedded pattern in the second measure of the Adagio (ex. 7-3), where the bass leaps among triad roots? Here embedding results from the placement of the functions within the meter. Corelli sounds the B-flat chords on strong parts of beats and the E-flat on the weak, precisely the reverse of the normal state of affairs (see chapter 8). (The same effect occurs in measure 5.) Furthermore, the functional rhythm to that point has

Ex. 7-3. Corelli, Concerto op. 6, no. 8, III, mm. 1–6.

Ex. 7-3. *Continued*

moved in slow half notes. Consistency, an important though not overriding consideration in analyzing a perception of rhythm, would suggest another half-note duration, and we can have it without sacrificing the obvious root movement in the bass by invoking an embedded pattern.

Consistency of pattern provides another set of embedded functions in the very next bar (m. 3). The cello begins its first important solo, an ar-peggiation of a strong progression: I–V. This turns out to be the first in-stance of a precisely composed harmonic-melodic sequence. Every triad pair shares that same root relationship of a perfect fourth that connects I to V, so even though there is no chromaticism, no explicit departure from the key of E-flat major, other tonal centers are suggested by the consistency of the sequential pattern. Those keys represent the triads C minor, A-flat major, and F minor on a more abstract level, all of which have subdominant function with respect to the principal key of E-flat. Just as the sentence had objects that contained subjects and verbs, so has Corelli constructed a com-plex subdominant that contains tonic and dominant functions embedded within it.

Pedal points, even when they occur in upper voices, are explicit agents of high-level harmonic functions. Tonic and dominant pedals, the most frequent by far, sound the tone that represents those functions while other voices move through completely integral progressions on a lower level. Examples of this embedding technique are legion. J. S. Bach uses exceedingly long pedals to structure his Domine Deus ritornello (ex. 5-5), and Vivaldi begins his "Winter" concerto with one (ex. 7-5). A more subtle example is the soprano C-sharp$_5$ in Bach's A Major Prelude (ex. 5-3, m.1). There it is not immediately apparent that we are hearing a pedal, for the pitch is neither tonic nor dominant degree, but it holds longer than any other voice thus far, while dissonant progressions pass below, and thus brings out the higher level progression.

A deceptive cadence frequently comprises an embedded function. We expect the great harmonic tension that Chopin has built up in his A-flat Etude (ex. 7-4) to resolve after the long dominant (mm. 27–28), but the cadence in measure 29 is deceptive, which the composer turns toward an even greater harmonic climax in the following measures. To communicate the effect of deception in a moment of harmonic resolution, a deceptive cadence must be heard in two ways: as a tonic function and as another, usually subdominant function. To achieve the first, the cadential chord, here the F minor triad (vi), draws on the context, the anticipation of a tonic created by the long dominant, and often clinches the disguise with a move to the tonic degree in the soprano melody. (In this case, the dominant

Ex. 7-4. Chopin, Etude op. 25, no. 1, mm. 26–29.

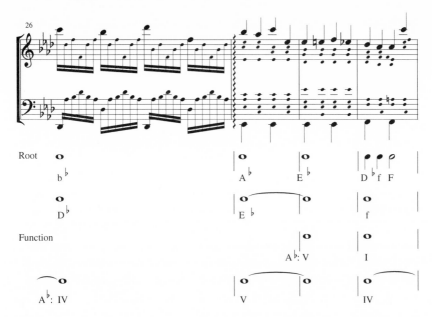

tension is so great that Chopin need not be so careful, and a descent to the mediant through the lower register suffices.) But unless there is something withheld from the resolution, then of course the cadence is not deceptive at all. Thus the substitution of some other triad containing the tonic note, thus the subdominant function on the higher level. The tonic function creating the cadential effect is embedded in the subdominant function that leads smoothly into the following climactic cadential run.

Surely the most explicit and frequent type of harmonic embedding occurs with the "borrowed," "applied," or "secondary" dominant. The very concept of deploying a dominant function triad belonging to a key other than the governing key while remaining within the latter all the while practically defines embedding.

Chromatically raised tones—new leading tones—may signal either a secondary dominant or a real modulation. The analyst must judge which interpretation is most faithful to the listening experience. This traditional problem has a long history; here I can only review quickly some of the more common considerations. The judgment affects the analysis of this dimension significantly, for modulations simply replace one tonal center with another, as in the Scarlatti, and the graph is unilevel. Secondary dominant interpretations entail embedded functions, and the graph is multilevel.

The case for secondary dominants is stronger whenever the key from which the dominant is borrowed (the object key) represents a strong function in the governing key. Consider two such passages in Corelli's Adagio (ex. 7-2), measures 5–6 and 13–14. The object keys are B-flat major and A-flat major. Since the triads B-flat major and A-flat major represent very strong dominant and subdominant functions in the governing key of E-flat major, it is very easy to hear these "little modulations" as elaborations of functions in E-flat major—as embedded functions. On the other hand, Scarlatti's choice of D minor as a harmonic goal near the beginning of his ritornello virtually eliminates a secondary dominant interpretation (ex. 7-1, m. 4). The D minor triad has very weak function in the key of G minor, so its sounding strikes the listener as a real change of key and sets the pattern for the rest of the ritornello.

Other considerations would include voice-leading and the presence or absence of the bass voice. In Corelli's movement the change from a leaping bass (ex. 7-2, mm. 9–11) to a conjunct bass alters the perception of a modulation passage into one that favors consistent reference to E-flat major, even though the overall texture of the writing remains the same. The writing in the solo first violin amplifies this effect, moving as it does conjunctly and climactically up to the high E-flat$_5$ tonic instead of away from it as before. Removing the bass entirely in measures 5–6 makes the functions implied by the solo violins seem weak, embedded in a higher-level dominant function represented by the last bass pitch, B-flat$_2$. Clearly, harmonic embedding is among the subtlest of compositional techniques, and convincing analysis can come only from experienced critical listening and judgment.

GRAPHING EMBEDDED FUNCTIONS

A modulation is graphed with one stream of duration symbols to show that the second key does not elaborate but displaces the first key in perception. An embedded syntax uses more than one stream of symbols according to the following conventions.

The governing key—the higher-level tonic, the key into which the elaborating syntax is embedded—must be declared in the higher-level, more abstract stream of duration symbols. In the Corelli movement (ex. 7-2) the governing key is E-flat major. The embedded rhythms are written above this abstract stream as a sign of embedding into it. This conforms with the arrangement of the root graphs: the more detailed surface motion is above the more abstract, slower motion.

An embedded progression can be a single chord, such as an embedded half cadence, but more commonly at least two chords form an embedded progression. There is no theoretical upper limit. Corelli's Adagio shows embedded progressions as short as two triads (mm. 13, 14) and as long as twelve (mm. 4–6).

Embedded functions are finite. This means that, as with the root progression graphs, the analyst is never obligated to carry out a functional level forever simply because one has started. The decision to continue a stream depends on the integrity of the progression, how audibly one function connects to another in that stream of motion. As shown in the Corelli, the great variety in the rhythmic profile of this apparently relentless music arises from embedded functions dropping out and reappearing as a means of sculpting the musical texture.

Analytic consistency demands somewhat stricter treatment of secondary dominant relations, a specific case of embedding. First, a single duration symbol and function (I, IV, or V) in the governing stream should represent the entire embedded progression created by the secondary dominant, and its duration should equal or surpass the summed duration of the embedded progression(s). So in measures 3–4 of the Corelli movement (ex. 7-2) the embedded progressions in C minor, A-flat major, and F minor last a total of six quarter notes. Since all have subdominant function within E-flat major, the governing key, they are subsumed by the expression IV under a half-note tied to the whole, an duration equal to the six quarters.

Second, the functions within the embedded progression are generally dominant and tonic, naturally, since it is dominant functions that are bor-

Ex. 7-5. Vivaldi, Concerto op. 8, no. 4, "Winter," I, mm. 1–12.

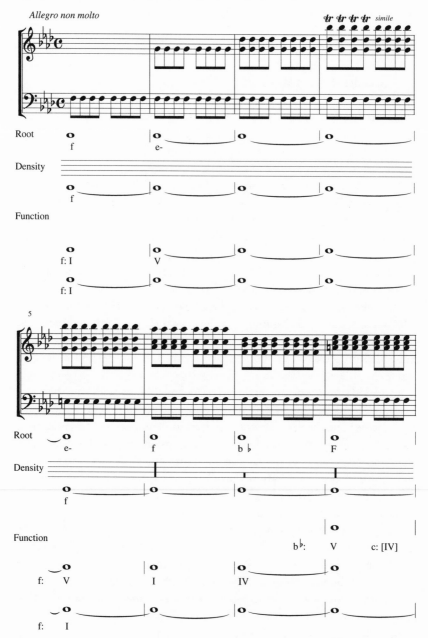

Ex. 7-5. *Continued*

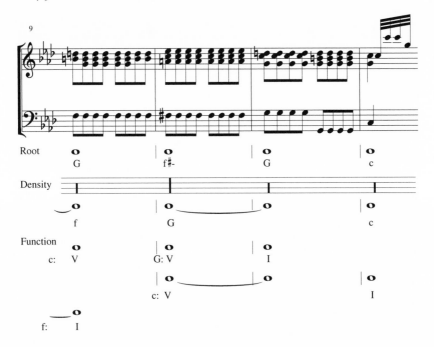

rowed. The single function that represents the whole embedding in the governing stream, however, is the function best represented by the triad corresponding to the object key. Measure 14 from Corelli has subdominant function (IV) on the higher level because the object key, or temporary tonic, is A-flat major, which corresponds to the strongly subdominant A-flat major triad in the governing key of E-flat major. Similarly, the next measure functions as a high-level dominant because another secondary dominant invokes a new object key, B-flat major, whose corresponding triad in the governing key is the strongest dominant. In general, the object keys of secondary dominant relations should have strong and unambiguous functions as "big triads" in the governing key.

The opening of Vivaldi's "Winter" concerto provides an excellent summary of harmonic embedding and its proper graphing (ex. 7-5). The insistent, almost menacing tonic pedal embeds the dominant function of the E diminished chord into the tonic from the start.[9] The bass moves off F$_3$ to the leading-tone E-natural in measure 5 but returns in the next bar; the conjunct voice-leading ensures the sustained perception of the pedal and the abstract tonic function it creates. From measure 6 the speed of root rhythm and function accelerate. In measure 8 Vivaldi elicits a third functional level, quite unusual in baroque music, by the dominant function of the F dominant seventh. This harmony implicates a new key, B-flat minor, for the first time as an embedded function. Because B-flat functions as a subdominant in the governing key of F minor, the second-level IV continues from measure 7. And because the bass is still pounding the F, the pedal continues, right on into measure 9. Now Vivaldi reinterprets the A-natural of measure 8 as a rising sixth degree in a new object key, C, identified by the new leading tone, B-natural. The bracketed IV shows the listener hearing Vivaldi reinterpret the F dominant seventh as a IV^7 in C minor. The second-level function disappears because the B-natural$_4$ following the A-natural makes F minor no longer tenable except as a pedal, already represented.

Measure 10 is the critical point in the buildup to the soloist's explosive entrance. The F pedal finally ceases; Vivaldi abandons the rock-solid stability of the third stream. For the first time, the two remaining functional streams move at once, and both change their tonal orientations at the same time. Dominant tension builds until the soloist resolves it, replacing it with lightning-fast animation of the textural rhythm.

The soloist's riveting entrance seems prepared, in part, by some kind of acceleration in harmonic rhythm, but it is not easy to point out. After all, the root harmonic rhythm does not appreciably accelerate after measure 6, so what creates the rise in tension? Moving away from the tonic is part of the story, but the pile-up of embedded relationships, the increased pace of "important things" happening, appears to be the only explanation. Now a commonsense interpretation of one graph is fine as far as it goes, but it is far better to have a real theory of interpretation, a systematic approach, some general principles that provide a means of comparing one piece with another in equivalent terms. With the dimensional analysis of harmonic rhythm now complete, interpretation is the next item on the agenda.

PART II.

Interpretation of Harmonic Rhythm

CHAPTER 8.

MATTERS OF INTERPRETATION

WHEN ONE finishes graphing all the individual dimensions, the analysis of a passage's harmonic rhythm is complete. Example 8-1 shows all the dimensions of harmonic rhythm in Arcangelo Corelli's Adagio from his "Christmas" Concerto, a movement that has illustrated almost every stage in the development of this analytical method. What can such a comprehensive graph teach us about the piece? How do we interpret all the various kinds of information in the graph?

The dimensional graph is an image of a piece that we can view in two general ways, diachronically and synchronically. The diachronic view is the moment-to-moment view that respects music's medium, the passage of time, a view that is interested in processes and changes in harmonic rhythm as we hear the piece from beginning to end. The synchronic view takes the piece, or any structure in it, as a whole event, a perceived Gestalt. Musical phrases, motives, and forms are among the ideas encountered with this approach.

Both views inform the perception of music, although usually different aspects of it, and both views are essential to many kinds of music analysis. Motivic analysis, for example, is diachronic as it describes the transformation of Corelli's original arpeggio in the solo violins (mm. 1–2) into a sequential version for the solo cello in the third measure but synchronic as it takes note of when the motive is heard and not heard, how it articulates the form of the movement and, indeed, even its definition of the arpeggio as a motive. The diachronic view may be likened to the panning of a video camera over a scene, the synchronic to a snapshot featuring a single object.

Ex. 8-1. Corelli, Adagio from Concerto op. 6, no. 8, "Christmas," with all dimensions of harmonic rhythm.

In many, perhaps most, perceptions the two views blend together. As we hear the cello sequence, we must process and recognize the motive in real time, a diachronic activity, while at the same time realizing that it resembles an earlier version, a much less temporal perception. So while it is possible and often useful to distinguish these two modes theoretically, it is not always wise to do so.

The dimensional graph of the Corelli piece has much to say from either point of view. Consider first some synchronic aspects.

Corelli begins with three statements of the arpeggio motive in the violins, all apparently identical in character. But the harmonic rhythm shows the third one already in transition. The shift to the A-flat harmony on the second beat of measure 2, subtly unsupported by the bass, creates another level of root motion that prepares the faster motion in three dimensions of the cadential progression and the next phrase. Here harmonic rhythm

Ex. 8-1. *Continued*

reveals an important change disguised by a more obvious identity. The Allegro, too, hides important irregularities with its false root movements of measures 10 and 13–14, an illusion carried off by Corelli's scoring of the texture, especially the bass voice.

The graph, still viewed as a synchronic "snapshot" of the movement, shows too the reverse illusion, the similarity that lies beneath an obvious musical contrast, such as the Allegro's transition back to the slower tempo. The cessation of the rapid motion of sixteenths and eighths (m. 19) is a sudden shock, tempered only by the expected resolution of the tonic triad, and the chords that follow are isolated by silences usually reserved for the most dramatic moments of a baroque opera. But the continuing streams of root and function rhythm show how consistent these dramatic flourishes are. Indeed, here the various dimensions are more united than at any other time in the whole movement. Corelli has invented a transition that con-

Ex. 8-1. *Continued*

cludes the section with conviction while preparing the slower tempo of the return, all without really interrupting the steadiness of the baroque pulse required by his musical language.

What about the most extraordinary parts of the snapshot, the passages most striking and memorable? The coda to the Adagio (mm. 30–33) is perhaps the most sublime passage in the entire "Christmas" Concerto. According to Corelli's da capo design for the movement, the coda is introduced as was the Allegro, with fairly quick harmonic rhythm (mm. 8, 29). But now the half-note dominant harmony finally moves to a tonic long enough to resolve it, in fact a tonic twice as long, created by an antiphonal arpeggiation in the violins on undaunted sixteenth notes that freezes the harmonic motion on the E-flat triad, the most sustained root and function heard in the movement to this point. Against this Gibraltar Corelli makes his greatest stroke, the bass descending from the tonic with the most poign-

Ex. 8-1. *Continued*

ant, slow dissonances against the violins in the same quarter-note speed that has characterized the root and function rhythm through most of the movement. It is a nostalgic reminiscence that disappears as soon as it is savored, leaving just two extremes of motion. As the violins now cascade to their tonic, the movement ends with the closing motive from measure 8, now doubly slow, set in a texture of nearly uniform harmonic rhythm. Thus the last measures summarize all the motile elements of the movement proper and yet, because of their radically slower root movement, sound like a coda from the onset, braking those same elements and coordinating harmonic tensions in a most graceful ending.

A virtue of harmonic rhythm noted from the very beginning is that it can give different impressions of a passage's speed even when note durations hold constant or, indeed, change in an opposite manner. A diachronic interpretation of a dimensional graph would be interested first of all in such

Ex. 8-1. *Continued*

impressions, which are for the most part fairly commonsense and obvious. It is not surprising that the slowest harmonic rhythm in the Corelli movement occurs in the first and last measures. In this way Corelli overlays a baroque facade of even motion throughout—mostly sixteenths in the textural rhythm—on top of an older Renaissance procedure in the more abstract harmonic rhythm by beginning slowly, generating tension in faster motions, and resolving it by slowing down again. Closer inspection explains less fundamental articulations, such as the strong phrase marker on the third beat of measure 5. The bass, first root, and first function dimensions all accelerate through the first two beats of the bar with high-density changes, so that the unified quarter-note duration, coordinated with the tonic resolution, comes off as a relaxation of pace. Corelli creates the opposite effect in the Allegro simply by changing the shape of the second-violin motive (m. 14). Immediately there is an acceleration in the contrapuntal phenomenal dimension, and nowhere else, giving just that much extra drive to the cadence.

Ex. 8-1. *Continued*

HARMONIC RHYTHM AND METER

The same passage deftly coordinates the function rhythm with the meter of the piece. Meter is a perception arising from regular patterns of changes and so is obviously connected with rhythm, and therefore harmonic rhythm. The interaction of meter and harmony, in fact, seems to have been the consideration that brought the whole issue of harmonic rhythm to theoretical consciousness in the writings of Rameau in the eighteenth century, when he advised against changing the harmony on the weak beat.

Rameau's advice, often repeated by later writers, implies that the meter of a passage is some kind of automatic, unstoppable force with which the harmonist had better reckon. The truth is more complicated. Harmonic changes do not only coordinate with metric patterns already present but help to establish and sustain those patterns. "Harmonic change is the single

Ex. 8-1. *Continued*

most powerful meter-producing factor," writes Joel Lester.[1] A significant harmonic change creates a phenomenal accent or emphasis that contributes mightily to the difference between a strong and a weak beat. Furthermore, there are cultural perceptions that link strong and weak beats to specific harmonic functions, namely, strong with tonic and weak, or upbeat, with dominant.[2] By exploiting these associations a composer can create a very clear and strong sense of meter from the first measure, as Corelli does at the beginning of the Adagio. By denying or reversing them, startling metric effects abound.

This is how Beethoven can characterize the governor Pizarro in his opera *Fidelio* as a puffed-up martinet, even before he appears on stage, by the way the march announces his arrival (ex. 8-2). Because the first two bass notes are unaccompanied, the listener takes them to be the roots of V and I in the key of B-flat. But that progression makes Beethoven's barring of the score seem wrong; surely the F_2 is an upbeat (weak), the B-flat$_2$ a downbeat (strong). There is no contradiction of this perception in the chim-

Ex. 8-1. *Continued*

ing woodwinds' figure, whose last chord seems to fall on another strong beat. The audience, blissfully unaware that the elegant march is metrically inverted, hears an exact repetition of this four-beat pattern and interprets it the same way.

The third measure sounds the bass and wind figures simultaneously, turning the bass pitch into a tonic triad factor. Though this second inversion normally has dominant function, it often occurs on the strong beat of a duple group, not the weak, so that it can lead to a root dominant on the weak beat. So perhaps we begin to doubt just a little bit the certainty of the F_2 bass pitch as upbeat. That doubt opens the door for Beethoven to introduce two identical root-position tonic triads, which broaden the ambiguity, since neither follows the expected V, then a half-diminished triad that could well be dominant function. This sounds like an upbeat in the wrong place, or an extra upbeat, or some other outlandish, Beethovenian syncopation, all of which is confirmed on the very next beat. By its resolution (downbeat association) of the E half-diminished chord and the long high A_5 in the oboe (agogic accent arising from comparatively long dura-

Ex. 8-2. Beethoven, "March," from no. 7, *Fidelio*, mm. 1–4.

tion), the A major triad resets the downbeat to its proper scored position at last. The opening of the march was a fake, and so is Pizarro.

Corelli's contrametric effect in his Allegro section is hardly so explicitly disorienting as Beethoven's; instead it contributes significantly to the perception of breathless forward motion. Consider once again those illusory triad changes in measures 10 and 13–14. What are they for? Why not have regular root rhythm? The answer is in the function graph. Were the C minor triad a half-note duration like all the rest, the following chord changes would shift one half note to the left, that is, they would sound one beat earlier. All the V functions would now fall on the upbeat and the I functions on the downbeat, the normal syntax in Corelli's musical language. But such an arrangement would create very strong articulations on each downbeat, too heavy for the forward motion the composer desires, and nearly breaking the passage into a series of tiny separate cadences. Corelli is after something subtler. By reversing the normal upbeat/dominant, downbeat/tonic syntax as Beethoven did, all the articulations, harmonic and metric, become weaker, forcing the listener to perceive the passage not as a series of tiny gestures but as a single propulsion.

Why then do we not sense a resetting of the downbeat, as we did in Beethoven? Why do we not begin to hear the tonic functions in G minor, F minor, and E-flat major as new downbeats? Actually, this perception would indeed occur if Corelli continued for much longer in the same manner as measures 11–13. But two things prevent the kind of radical reinterpretation of the meter we hear in Beethoven's march.

First, Corelli's harmonic context is entirely different. Beethoven's false meter depends entirely on the fact we hear those bass pitches, unaccompanied, as the first notes of the piece. There is no sense of beat yet, never mind which is weak and strong. The audience interprets as best it can, according to its knowledge of Beethoven's musical language. Corelli's Allegro, on the other hand, begins as a strongly articulated authentic cadence prepared by the Adagio. There is not the slightest doubt that the first E-flat triad in the Allegro is the downbeat, and this is confirmed when the next tonic function, now in C minor, falls as expected. And if the performers adopt a "unified beat" approach to the movement, equating the eighth-note of the Adagio with the half note of the Allegro, they further encourage this normal metric perception.

Now a well-known and widely accepted principle of perception says that once a sensory pattern achieves stability, perceivers strongly prefer to continue organizing the sensory stimuli in the same way.[3] Beethoven, by offering only isolated bass notes, never makes the implied meter strong enough to prevent the listener from questioning it by the third measure. Corelli presents, by contrast, an incontrovertible meter. After measure 10, listeners will resist any change, unless there are overpowering contrametric accents or a significant number of milder accents, as Corelli has, and we give up resisting and reset.

This he does not allow. The next illusory triad change lands an inverted E-flat triad on the first beat of measure 14—ignoring Rameau's advice, by the way—where we have been expecting it for some time. That, another rescoring of the orchestra parts, and a new motive in the second violin all create a significant phenomenal accent to reassure us that the meter, while weakened, has not changed. Then, as he begins a new round of metric reversals, the second prevention, a new stream of functional harmonic rhythm, arises, which changes always on the first beat of the notated bar, preserving the forward motion of the whole passage without metric disorientation.

Harmonic rhythm, harmonic function, and meter are all intimately related in rather complex feedback relationships. Corelli's contrametric deployment of dominant and tonic functions is not simply a matter of using an established meter to weaken the functions; the repressed functions also begin to weaken the sense of meter at the same time. Neither effect is absolutely prior to the other; both act at once to influence the perception of the other. That is why Beethoven's march is so strange. Most traditional pieces begin with functions and meter highly coordinated, immediately reinforcing one another to establish a clear meter and key as quickly as possible. Once those essential contexts are set, effects of harmonic and metric ambiguity have something against which to play.

If this relationship is so intimate, might there be a "harmonic meter" that arises from regular chord changes, somehow distinct from the "normal" meter of a passage, analogous to harmonic rhythm, which is a rhythmic perception distinct from the surface note rhythm?

In traditional theories, meter requires two elements: beats of consistent length and a regular pattern of accenting those beats.[4] Harmony rarely supplies either. Since the whole matter of harmonic rhythm is grounded in harmonic changes, a "harmonic meter" would demand that harmony change at some consistent time durations—the harmonic beat—other than those marked by the attack points of the melodies that constitute the texture. This is impossible, since it is the melodic changes that create the harmonic ones. Indeed, the fascination of harmonic rhythm is in the variety of harmonic lengths, not in their consistency. If there is no "harmonic beat" other than the one coincident with the beat of the texture, then there can be no regular accented beat except one coincident with the texture. Is it possible, then, that a "harmonic meter" could then exist, if not independently, at least out of phase with the normal textural meter?

In a limited fashion Beethoven and Corelli accomplish this, but the sensation of it is very brief indeed. The effect is a special kind of syncopation, a sustained metric disturbance. If extended too far, such harmonic tricks simply establish a new meter altogether, resetting the downbeat. Harmonic rhythm can produce extraordinary contrametric effects, but it does not create its own "harmonic meter."

The dimensional graph does not explicitly announce contrametric effects. They are an interpretation, validated by listening, of course, made by someone observing how the harmonic changes relate to the prevailing meter or, if there is none established, how they create one.[5] The same is true of the other interpretations made of Corelli—the diversities of motion hidden under apparent consistencies, the reverse at the conclusion of the Allegro passage, the convincing dissonance of the coda. All are criticisms that the graph makes possible by itself, with only the help of common sense and good musical intuition, and all grant some insight into Corelli's lovely movement through the perspective of harmonic rhythm.

Still, if harmonic rhythm is truly a multidimensional aspect of music, greater contributions should be made, particularly toward a diachronic view of the music, from an understanding of the interaction of those many dimensions. Is there any difference in musical effect, for example, between a passage that shows many active dimensions and levels and another that shows but few? Does it matter if there is a great disparity in speed between dimensions? Why, in the Corelli movement, does neither the fastest duration nor the slowest ever dominate the entire graph at any moment, but rather, when the dimensions do move more or less homorhythmically, they compromise on a medial value, as in measure 5? Is there any link between the kind of harmonic tension we associate with functions and the rhythmic tension of harmonic changes?

In general, it is the universal aspect of musical tension and resolution that should be at the heart of an interpretation of harmonic rhythm. Tension in this sense is any musical quality that communicates or otherwise leads the listener to expect more music to follow: forward motion in time; resolution is its opposite: cessation and stability. Surely, rhythm, the very embodiment of motion in music, mirrors the particular kinds of musical tension and resolution arising from changes rapid and slow. But harmonic rhythm promises more. In the western tradition, harmony is intimately linked with the syntax of musical languages, and it is one of the two primary cognitive functions of musical syntax to shape, control, and deploy musical tension and resolution.[6] Thus an analysis of harmonic rhythm should say quite a lot about the dynamics of a passage, not just the gross articulations but also the interactions and varieties of musical tensions experienced in the act of listening.

To interpret the dimensional graph in this way requires a few new principles.

CHAPTER 9.

THE SPEED OF HARMONIC

RHYTHM

*T*O UNDERSTAND tension and resolution in harmonic rhythm, consider the moment in a piece of music when resolution is complete and tension is nil: the end. What is required to compose a satisfactory ending? Broadly taken, the question evokes all kinds of aesthetic considerations of form, proportion, balance, and so on, and indeed, ending is often the most difficult aspect of composition to master. But considering only the purely technical requirements of the last moment, the essential thing is that all change—all motions of tones—must cease. A few extraordinary pieces such as Alban Berg's *Lyric Suite* attempt to do without a definitive ending. In this case the viola of his quartet repeats a decrescendo ostinato figure until it is inaudible, suggesting infinite continuity, but traditionally, composers want listeners to know with absolute certainty when the composition is over. Stopping all motion is their unmistakable sign of ending: no more pitch onsets, no more textural or harmonic rhythm of any kind.[1]

This fact merely illustrates a principle of musical tension taken for granted probably the world over: motion creates musical tension, and the faster the motion (the more changes per unit of time) the greater the tension. This is only one kind of musical tension, to be sure, one of many kinds, but it is a fundamental kind. The very conception of tension as that quality of music that communicates more music to follow, forward motion in time, begets this principle as a virtual tautology.

The Bach prelude in example 9-1 has an absolutely consistent motor rhythm of eighth notes (see textural/phenomenal graph), but other har-

Ex. 9-1. J. S. Bach, A Major Prelude from *The Well-Tempered Clavier*, vol. 2, mm. 1–6.

Ex. 9-1. *Continued*

monic dimensions show much more rhythmic variety. The peak of tension as pure motion occurs in measures 4 and 5, when all the dimensions attain their fastest speeds. Viewed synchronically, taking all the dimensions as a whole texture, this is the fastest harmonic rhythm of the piece so far, and its relaxation at the downbeat of measure 6 articulates an important half cadence. Bach employs a very simple idea here, albeit in sophisticated fashion, to shape the first big harmonic phrase.

One advantageous property of this kind of harmonic tension from the composer's standpoint is its pinpoint control. Accelerations and decelerations can be imperceptibly gradual, hurried, or explosive, with all grades in between. There is no technical preparation required for speeding or slowing, although there may indeed be aesthetic requirements. Bach shapes the phrase with his gentle acceleration in the prelude, while Corelli accelerates suddenly to articulate a whole new section in his Adagio (ex. 8-1, mm. 8–9).

A second property of harmonic speed, deriving from harmonic rhythm's many dimensions, is complexity of effect. No dimension in Bach's prelude moves faster than the phenomenal, whose steady stream of eighths seems placidly unaffected by the pushing and pulling in the other dimensions. But this fleet surface does not determine a consistent overall perception of harmonic motion in the music. Evidently the speed of harmonic rhythm can be "colored," depending on the dimensions that change or remain constant. Indeed, that is one of its abiding attractions.

In fact, the color of harmonic speed has a surprisingly singular quality. Critics and composers such as Walter Piston speak of one passage having faster harmonic rhythm than another and even of entire musical languages, such as the baroque, being characterized by fast harmonic rhythm in comparison to the romantic. Surely this is not because baroque composers make sure that all their harmonic dimensions always move more rapidly than all those of romantic composers, in the same aggregate sense that Bach's measure 5 is faster than measure 2. The shimmering Chopin Etude op. 25, no. 1 (ex. 9-4), stands out immediately as a contradictory case, and there are thousands of others. Thinking back to the musical passages studied earlier, impressions of speeding and slowing are not reflected in all the dimensions. The illusory triad changes in the Allegro section of the Corelli come to mind once again (ex. 8-1, mm. 10, 14). Why does the music not sound immediately slower there? What is it that creates the singular impression of a harmonic speed in a passage that has many harmonic dimensions? And if a perception of singular speed is primary, why do the other harmonic dimensions matter?

THE FOCAL STREAM

In a dimensional analysis of harmonic rhythm, each dimension contributes its own particular perspective, without which the picture of the harmonic texture is incomplete. In that sense, then, each dimension, each stream of harmonic-rhythmic change, is important as long as it is present. But that does not mean that the listener attends to each one with equal concentration, that each stream is equally salient in the listener's perception.

Why and how humans attend to certain stimuli more than others are cognition problems just beginning to be understood, but certain well-accepted principles, some obvious, others surprising, can clarify this theory of harmonic rhythm.

No one can listen and fully understand two different conversations at the same time. Reading a book while driving is asking for trouble. Detecting errors in a chorus rehearsal becomes more difficult as the number of voices increases. Common experiences like these, as well as laboratory evidence, demonstrate that the capacity to maintain sophisticated percepts in full awareness is limited.[2] Researchers have located processing bottlenecks at the point when raw percepts are introduced to cognition and also at higher-level cognitive representation. The former may affect how we understand rapid polyphony, perhaps enforcing a kind of quick switching of attention from one voice to another. The latter, central bottleneck constrains sophisticated judgments and responses, but it may be eased by practice and familiarity on one hand and by executing tasks that occupy different cognitive channels and modules on the other. Thus, experienced drivers can carry on sophisticated conversations in the car because many of the stimulus and response patterns of driving have become routine and because driving involves sight and motor response, faculties different from those required for language.[3]

Limited attention means we must choose what to focus on. Common experience suggests that this choice is largely voluntary and conscious, but it is not always so. A classic example of diverted attention is the hearing of one's name. It seems equally hard to ignore fortissimo brass entrances.[4] In an activity demanding sustained concentration such as music, certain aspects seem more worthy of attention. Indeed, that is the principle behind the notion of homophonic texture: one voice enjoys a perceptual salience at the expense of the others. Generalizing about which aspects are likely to grab the listener's attention is tantamout to asking "What is so interesting about music?" The relevant factors are many and complex. It is enough to assume at this point that in the typical attentive act of listening, the particular focus wanders where it may, following whatever attractor is most salient at the moment.

The "choice" need not be entirely exclusive, and indeed research has shown that it rarely is so.[5] While the last question from the driver's interlocutor may be in the center of awareness, events on the road remain in the periphery—one hopes—at some lower level of awareness. An unexpected maneuver in the left lane momentarily can reverse the situation and delay the driver's response to his friend's question. Similarly, the endlessly repeating arpeggiation in Chopin's etude is probably not at the forefront of most listeners' experiences, but they are certainly aware, at some level, of its harmonic import. Otherwise no one would notice when it suddenly ceases at the prelude's end.

The perception of harmonic rhythm itself, in competition with beautiful melodies and so many other fascinations of a musical language, probably floats on this periphery of awareness much of the time. But insofar as it does affect experience, the reason that harmonic rhythm conveys a singular impression of speed, despite all the diversity in the different dimensions, is that the listener attends chiefly to only one speed: the *focal stream*. The other speeds of harmonic dimensions color this perception from the background.

A rough comparison with speech, another multilevel sound phenomenon like music, may clarify this effect. Consider listening to the following two sentences, spoken at normal speed.

Fred strained his hamstring and screamed. (30 phonemes)
Kay pulled a muscle and yelled. (18 phonemes)

Both sentences say similar things, have similar syntax, have equal numbers of syllables to pronounce, and require about two seconds to execute. At this speed there is no sense of hurry or exaggerated slowness about either one, yet the first one requires the perceiving mind to process the elementary sounds of English, its phonemes, at a rate over 50 percent faster than the second (see the counts for comparison).[6] Why is there no sense of strain in hearing the first one? Because there is rarely any need to attend to individual phonemes with a high degree of conscious awareness. Much of the processing work is automatic—so much so, in fact, that if one or two phonemes are mispronounced, coughed over, or otherwise obscured, no notice is taken.[7] Instead, awareness is riveted on another level of comprehension: the words. The analogy is not precise, of course, since in music the individual sounds matter a great deal, but the analogy demonstrates how an attention limits conscious awareness of phenomena in a complex temporal percept without losing it altogether.

Awareness is just as variable in the more abstract realm of semantic content. Consider these passages:

God created man in the image of himself, in the image of God he created
    him, male and female he created them. (Gen. 1:27)
The Lord God said, "It is not good that the man should be alone. I will
    make him a helpmate."(Gen. 2:18)

Once again the two passages have similar length and syntactic complexity, but the semantic content of the first is lower. Despite this difference, the first sentence does not sound particularly laggard or the second particularly hurried, when pronounced at the same comfortable speed, about 7–8 seconds. Attention is not focused on the rate of ideas presented but on the rate and sound of the words spoken. This does not mean that there is no effect of highly repetitive speech, only that its effect is subliminal in certain contexts.

The focal stream of harmonic rhythm, then, is the series of durations of harmonic changes represented by at least one dimension corresponding to the locus of the listener's greatest attention. More simply, it is the speed of harmonic change that we are most aware of in the listening experience.

Some further delimitation. The focal stream is not anything of constant speed, like the tactus or "conducting" beat that corresponds with the tempo of the music. Nor must it be constantly represented by a single dimension throughout a passage, although it could be. Often the focal stream shifts from one dimension to another, and, if more than one dimension move together, it can be represented by several of them. But it must be represented by at least one real dimension. The focal stream is not a virtual motion or articulation, as meter can sometimes be. There must be changes in sounding phenomena somewhere in the dimensional analysis that correspond to our perception of a singular harmonic rhythm.

Returning to the Bach prelude (ex. 9-1), the focal stream at the beginning is brisk, represented almost unanimously by the bass pitch and the first levels of root and function rhythm. Then it brakes suddenly in the second measure, still best shown in the first root and function dimensions. These accelerate rapidly in the next bar until, rather mysteriously, the focal stream shifts to the second-level root and function dimensions and remains there through measure 5.

In Corelli's Adagio the focal stream allies itself quite consistently with the first level of root/quality rhythm (see ex. 8-1), which begins very slowly with half notes, then accelerates to steady quarters for the cello sequence, then finally moves in eighth-note durations when approaching the first cadence. In the Allegro section it is the bass voice, always moving in half notes, that captures our attention, which is why the doubly long triads in measures 10 and 14 do not restrain the forward motion of the piece.

How do we determine which dimension(s) of harmonic rhythm occupies our attention? Again, there is no magic formula that infallibly selects a focal stream to unanimous agreement, but there are a number of criteria that should support an intuitive judgment.

First, the more dimensions that contribute to the focal stream the better, and the stronger the choice. Both the Bach and Corelli graphs show numerous places where more than one dimension move at the same speed. This means that different harmonic aspects are changing simultaneously and, like a crowd of people moving or chanting in unison as opposed to one individual, they are much more likely to capture the attention of the listener.

Second, the listener attends to streams of events that offer strong structural coherence, events that make sense following one another. When listening to speech the auditor focuses on the individual words rather than the individual sounds or the general ideas because that is where the salient grammar, the syntax of the language, obtains. Analogously, the functional relations we learn to hear among the various triads of a key bind them together much more tightly and predictably than, say, the succession of phenomenal chords.

That is one reason why, in the Bach and Corelli and thousands of other traditional passages, the rhythms of root and function unite in the focal stream. Furthermore, the changes of harmonic function control a significant kind of musical tension that drives the whole musical dynamic. The move to the subdominant in Bach's third measure and the resolution of the long dominant in Corelli's sixth are clearly profiled, intrinsically interesting harmonic events, like the twists of a good plot. Such harmonic changes make up a large part of the reason why we listen to such music in the first place, so naturally their demand for our attention is almost irresistible.

Part of musical coherence is consistency. Notice how the focal stream in the Corelli changes its speed very gently, never by a factor greater than two. Such a smooth transition reassures the listener that the attended stream is indeed continuous. On the other hand, sometimes, as when Corelli moves into the Allegro or, more subtly, in Bach's second measure, there is no choice but to change, simply because there is nothing else of substance happening.

Another part of musical coherence is stability, which is perhaps another way of describing structural strength. In the Mozart piano sonata graphed in example 9-2, there is much rhythmic variety among the dimensions. The best choice for the focal stream at the beginning, however, is the whole-note motion represented by the second-level root and function motions. For one thing, they are the only two dimensions moving homorhythmically, consistently together. Perhaps more important, however, is that they change on the downbeat of each measure, making a strong pattern that enjoys the stability of the meter. The other dimensions, particularly the contrapuntal phenomenal, the bass pitch, and the first-level root, reflect Mozart's offbeat conception for his thematic material, no trivial matter, but such offbeat changes, along with the great variety of durations involved, make it a more difficult pattern for the listener to assimilate. The wisdom of choosing the second-level root is born out in the later measures, when it accelerates into easily perceptible progressions that organize an even more wildly syncopated first-level.

A third criterion is absolute speed. Attention involves the working memory, of course, that model of our cognition that stores fresh sensory information for immediate interpretation. Psychologists estimate that information can remain there in a raw, uninterpreted state for perhaps two to four seconds. Thus there is a lower limit on the speed of the focal stream; if the harmonic changes are too slow we cannot remember them well enough to make sense of them. That is why the focal stream at the beginning of Vivaldi's "Winter" Concerto is at the very surface, the phenomenal harmonic rhythm (ex. 10-3). All others are either motionless or moving too slowly to be processed as a continuous sound pattern. When the roots begin to change at every whole note in measure 6, as the phenomenal rhythm did before, their dimension takes over the focal stream.

On the other hand, one experiment showed that listeners could not recognize famous melodies when presented too fast.[8] There is probably an

Ex. 9-2. Mozart, Piano Sonata K. 333, I, mm. 1–9.

Ex. 9-2. *Continued*

upper limit to the speed of the focal stream, too. The happy medium required here brings to mind the tactus, or conducting beat, traditionally thought to reflect the human pulse. Although the focal stream is not constant like the tactus, the preference, all other things being equal, is for a speed close to the speed of the tactus.[9]

In short, the focal stream should be easy to find; after all, it is the center of attention. The general concern in all these criteria is the salience of the motion whose clarity and musical attraction cry out to be heard consciously. A sense of the focal stream is perhaps what motivated Walter Piston's original concept of harmonic rhythm as the motion of triads, for indeed, in the traditional musical language that he described, the changes in triads and their functions very often constitute the most salient aspect of the harmonic rhythm.

SOME DATA ANALYSIS OF THE
FOCAL STREAM

Once found, the focal stream provides a kind of standard for harmonic rhythm, a means of evaluating the individual dimensions and of comparing one passage with another. A tiny sampling of such comparisons is shown in table 9-1.

The table shows two ways of measuring and comparing the focal streams from various passages. The first way is to compare them with the textural rhythm, which stands for the absolute upper limit on harmonic rhythm (see chapter 2). No dimension of harmonic rhythm can be faster than the rhythm of the texture. Thus the maximum focal stream/texture ratio is 1.00, and this limit creates a certain kind of scale for the harmonic rhythm of a passage. Remember, however, that the textural rhythm is itself variable. The ratios for the Corelli Allegro passage, for instance, might imply that the focal stream moves rather slowly most of the time, since the average (0.14) is close to the slowest rate of changes for the passage (0.12). The highest ratio, the maximum 1.00, falsely implies an enormous increase in speed somewhere, for in the transition near the end, it is the textural rhythm that slows radically and matches the focal harmonic rhythm.

Actually the harmonic rhythm of the Allegro sounds quite consistent, which is shown in the second set. Here the focal stream is compared to a constant value for the passage, the tactus, or conducting beat. The disadvantage of this statistic is that there is no maximum ratio, but the 1.00 ratios across the board for Corelli reveal the remarkable consistency of the focal stream in the Allegro passage.

We can interpret such data for musical characteristics. A low focal/texture ratio indicates many rhythmic events in the musical texture for each harmonic event; in short, a lot of surface activity, brilliant virtuoso

Table 9-1. Analysis of Harmonic Speeds in Five Passages: Duration ratios of the focal stream to the textual rhythm and of the focal stream to the tactus.

	Focal/Texture			Focal/Tactus		
	Lowest	Average	Highest	Lowest	Average	Highest
Bach, prelude	0.11	0.50	1.00	0.33	1.50	3.00
Corelli, Adagio	0.12	0.34	1.00	0.25	0.58	1.00
Corelli, Allegro	0.12	0.14	1.00	1.00	1.00	1.00
Mozart, K. 333	0.09	0.17	0.50	0.25	0.43	1.00
Chopin	0.02	0.04	0.08	0.12	0.26	0.50

writing, musical glitter. Thus it is no surprise to read that Chopin's piece, with its constant shimmer of arpeggios, has by far the lowest average (0.04). Bach's prelude stands out from the crowd of five here for the speed of its focal stream; it has both the highest focal/texture average and the highest focal/tactus average. Yet the prelude also has the greatest range of speeds: the fastest harmonic rhythm is nine times faster than the slowest; in the other compositions the fastest harmonic rhythm is only about four times faster than the slowest. As we read down the list, the averages tend to drop, supporting the intuitive perception that, in general, classical and romantic harmonic languages have slower harmonic rhythm than the baroque. A myriad of similar empirical arguments quickly materialize from such tabulations of data, but of course samples must be much, much larger before any such claims could be serious. Here we can only point out what might come of studying the focal stream.

But Bach's prelude also presents a counterintuitive reading in the fourth measure. Here the focal stream has shifted to the second-level root/quality rhythm, supported most of the time by the functional rhythm and the bass pitch rhythm. The intuition is that this measure begins the most intense part of the passage; how is it that the focal stream of harmonic rhythm could be slower than it was before? Tension should be less, the music more relaxed. Part of the answer to this paradox is to remember that the sheer speed of harmonic rhythm provides only one kind of musical tension, one among many that interact and contradict each other in infinite complexity. But considering the relation of the focal stream to the other harmonic dimensions provides more positive answers.

MUSICAL TENSIONS OF THE
FOCAL STREAM

How does the focal stream relate and interact with the rest of the harmonic texture? There are three general cases. The first is that of the *phenomenal focal stream*. In this case the focal stream is represented by one or more of the faster harmonic dimensions of the passage. It corresponds to immediate sense perception, with minimal interpretation—thus the term "phenomenal"—and the slower dimensions are heard as abstractions of its motion.[10] The focal stream in measures 1 and 3 of the Bach prelude are classic examples: it moves nearly as fast as the textural rhythm itself, which is as fast as any harmonic motion can move.

The second case is that of the *abstract focal stream*, as in the fourth and fifth measures of the prelude. Here the slower dimensions represent the focal stream and the faster ones elaborate its motion.

These are relative terms. A phenomenal focal stream will rarely be the fastest one possible in the texture; rather, the textural and phenomenal dimensions will usually set the fastest pace. And an abstract focal stream need not be represented by the slowest dimension; it need only be slower relative to most of the other salient dimensions.

Recall now the definition of the focal stream as that motion that best captures the listener's conscious attention and the assumption that such attention has limited capacity. A reasonable hypothesis, as the next step, is that multiple salient streams of motion create greater musical tension than singular ones simply because they cost more effort to attend to. Of course, such attention must be musically rewarding, not just encountering noise or senseless sound sequences, according to the nature of the musical language in question. So, to be more specific, musical tension from harmonic rhythm increases directly with fruitful effort of attending to it—a kind of "process tension."

This process tension is distinct in quality from the kind that comes of sheer speed of harmonic rhythm, the raw motion that concerned this discussion at the beginning. Process is related to speed because it derives from forward motion in the music, but it arises more directly from competing patterns set before the listener by the harmonic texture. How fast they move absolutely is secondary with regard to process tension. And of course neither of these tensions of harmonic rhythm has anything to do with the harmonic tension produced by harmonic function, such as the syntactic tendency of a dominant for its tonic, to use the most obvious example. Highly skilled composers may coordinate functional tensions with the rhythmic most admirably, but they remain a distinct kind of tension.

Generally, the phenomenal focal stream already has more speed tension built right into it than the abstract focal stream. Thus we feel a relaxation of motion in measure 2 of the prelude and an acceleration in measure 3. But if it is true that the focal stream shifts to the more abstract level of root rhythm in measure 4 and itself becomes a more abstract stream, why should there not be a sense of relaxation there too? Well, there is some relaxation, in the sense of pure speed and in another kind of musical tension yet to be explored (chapter 10). But in another respect, the passage brings on a peak of excitement, because, all things being equal, the abstract focal stream generates more process tension than does the phenomenal.[11]

When a listener attends to a phenomenal focal stream, other harmonic events such as high-level root movement and function move more slowly. They do register in awareness, indeed, but only once in a while. Because they are almost always easily recognized, strongly profiled, downbeat events, they can be quickly categorized by the mind and put on the back burner of consciousness until the next comes along. The opening bars of the prelude present a high-level A triad with tonic function and then a high-level E triad with dominant function. They are essential articulations to be sure, but we need not fixate on them. There are more lively things to attend to.

When attention is captured by an abstract focal stream, then the other harmonic events move faster since they elaborate it. Even while they remain in the background of consciousness, they relentlessly pester for attention at a great rate. Thus, in Bach's fourth and fifth bars, the eighth-note chords, moving with lower density and tenuous functional relations with one another, never undermine the focus on the dotted-quarter motions whose functional syntax and sequential pattern tightly binds them together and makes them salient. But they threaten every moment to do so, and so the attention given them is unquestionably greater. Despite the reduction in the speed of the focal stream, another tension seems more acute, certainly different, and completes the dynamic shaping of Bach's first long phrase.

While never displacing the focal stream, the first-level root and function rhythms of this point in the prelude, at times, compete with it on a nearly equal basis. The rise of the soprano melody at the end of the fourth bar, leading to a high tonic pitch on the strongest beat in the vicinity, supported by a complete syntactic form (I–IV–V–I), is such a moment, like a burning ember that flares briefly before subsiding into a glimmer. For this brief time, conscious attention is truly divided. Such a condition persisting through a passage is the third general case of stream interaction: the *bifocal stream*.

Which dimension represents the focal stream of harmonic rhythm at the very end of Corelli's Adagio (ex. 8-1, mm. 30–33), in the coda? The root motion leading into it (m. 29), comparatively fast eighths and quarters, connects best with the descending bass since its speed is consistent. But because the violins cascade in their relentless E-flat major arpeggio (m. 30), one cannot take the bass seriously as a continuation of the progression. Harmonic syntax demands that attention move to the much slower root rhythm. One measure later there is unanimity in all dimensions except the phenomenal; the conflict disappears. For the one moment in the whole composition, however, the focal stream splits. This amplifies those marvelous dissonances in the bass because we cannot take our ears off them, cannot dismiss the conjunct melody as mere voice-leading. The most luminous moment in the movement owes something of its special tension to a bifocal stream of harmonic rhythm.

The bifocal stream creates more process tension, all things being equal, than either the phenomenal or abstract focal streams, by the same logic. It is akin to following two conversations at once, but the polyphony is syntactically coordinated, one stream with another, and we can just accomplish it with a lot of effort. The effort itself provides one kind of tension for such moments.

Occasionally a bifocal stream may dominate an entire passage, giving an impression of extreme contrapuntal density and intricacy. In Bach's fugal passage introducing Kyrie I of the *Mass in B Minor* (ex. 9-3), the focal stream begins with only the second-level root and function dimensions, but when the bass accelerates in measure 6 and the oboes leap from the A-sharp$_4$ in measure 7 to course downward in that expressive arch that harmonizes the bass, the faster chords become equally salient, and from then on the stream is bifocal. The criteria for making such an interpretation are the same as

Ex. 9-3. J. S. Bach, Kyrie I from the *Mass in B Minor*, mm. 5–11.

Ex. 9-3. *Continued*

for a single focal stream: structural stability, coherence, and a speed close to the tactus, but in this passage the criteria consistently point to two different speeds of motion (except in measure 8, where there is a brief convergence to highlight the answering subject). Even the density graph confirms both. What is amazing about Bach's counterpoint here is how both levels of progression in measures 9–11 make perfectly comprehensible syntax. Each triad leads grammatically to the next, no matter whether brief or long, an astounding feat of coordination.

Bach's Kyrie introduction confronts the listener with a constant barrage of intense harmonic rhythm, a relentless challenge to the listener's attention. Chopin, by contrast (ex. 9-4), uses the bifocal stream to shape a phrase, to intensify a particular moment, as did Corelli in his Adagio and Bach in his A Major Prelude. It is quite clear how Chopin uses the sheer speed of

Ex. 9-4. Chopin, Etude op. 25, no. 1, mm. 1–8.

harmonic rhythm to build up tension in the etude's first eight-bar phrase. The focal stream at first is phenomenal; its locus is in the first-level root and function. In the fifth bar it shifts to the second-level root; the quarter-note progressions in measure 6 seem more coloristic than syntactic, and the halfnotes are consistent with the preceding motion. Now the focal stream is abstract, and there is a slight increase in tension. The embedded functions, however, foreordain new complexity, which takes hold immediately in measures 7 and 8. Now the progressions and functions at both speeds are strong; one cannot ignore either. Suddenly in measure 8 the harmonic texture clears. The more abstract dimensions brake to a whole note, and embedded functions disappear. The first-level root pauses gently on the dominant triad, a half note retarding its own momentum. Only the contrapuntal phenomenal rhythm supplies the necessary connection to the next phrase. Once again, the process tension of the bifocal stream has given Chopin's music a delicate but unmistakable climax.

Ex. 9-4. *Continued*

That clearing of independent motion in measure 8 is something that occurs in many of the musical examples interpreted so far. That it coincides with a major articulation is no chance effect, for the control of the different motions in the harmonic texture as a whole is the source of the other principal kind of musical tension generated by harmonic rhythm, the tension of harmonic independence.

CHAPTER 10.

INDEPENDENCE IN HARMONIC

RHYTHM

*T*HE PRINCIPLE of harmonic speed derives reasonably from the simple fact that all motion must cease at the end of a composition. Recall this notion of a satisfactory ending, that moment in a piece of music when resolution is complete and tension is nil, for it requires something else of the harmony. When a polyphonic composition ends, the individual contrapuntal voices achieve homorhythm. Durations match up; the melodies move together. It is true that in some pieces this occurs with absolute unanimity only with the very last chord, but in many others it happens earlier. The principle of harmonic independence hypothesizes, then, that a particular kind of musical tension rises with increasing rhythmic independence of the dimensions of harmonic rhythm, called *divergence*, and resolves with increasing unanimity of the dimensions, *convergence*.

On first meeting one might think that this principle is a logical consequence of harmonic speed: if all motion ceases, it is surely inevitable that all the contrapuntal voices end up together, even if it is only sustaining the last chord. The mutual influence of these two principles is certainly strong, but the resolution of convergence is not quite a corollary of harmonic speed. It is possible for contrapuntal voices to simply drop out of the texture altogether as a piece winds down. Thus, when motion ceases, there is no unanimity because voices have disappeared.

This almost never happens in music composed before 1900 and rarely in music composed afterward. Try to come up with a motet, cantata, or oratorio where all the singers do not sing at the end or a quartet or symphony where all the players do not play the last chord. Even keyboard music nearly always demands a full sonority for closing.[1] Haydn's "Farewell" Symphony, no. 45, whose finale eliminates instruments one by one as the variations proceed, is the exception that proves the rule; it is famous because it is so odd. An aesthetic law rules most of the Western tradition: satisfactory ending requires a full texture. The principle of harmonic independence is really a principle of counterpoint, from which harmonic rhythm, of course, derives.

In musical languages that depend heavily on contrapuntal texture, such as that of the high Renaissance, different voices may end at different times (ex. 10-1).[2] Josquin ends his monumental motet with a plagal cadence, which begins the moment one of the voices achieves the tonic pitch and sustains it through the end. Here it is the second tenor (m. 65), who is joined by the cantus (top), bassus, and first tenor, filling out the last triad in measure 67. Finally the altus arrives at its last note, also a tonic. Despite the earlier

Ex. 10-1. Josquin, Motet "Miserere mei, Deus," III, mm. 65–68.

endings, the piece as a whole can end only when all motion has ceased, producing a unanimity at the last among the five voices. Harmonic independence here requires the plagal cadence as a kind of contrapuntal cushion, absorbing the forward momentum of the texture until each individual part is exhausted.

Simpler harmonic textures that characterized more popular part-songs and hymns of this period could make cadences more directly, almost instantly. Example 10-2 shows an early form of Protestant hymnody. By reading the dimensional graph vertically, one can see how remarkably homorhythmic the various dimensions are most of the time. What little divergence there is clears up immediately before each cadence. The most divergence—still not very much—occurs in the middle of the last phrase, a tiny climax near the end.

So here are two rather extreme cases of harmonic convergence and divergence. Music rarely clings to one texture or the other for very long, of course; to vary the harmonic rhythm and its tension through the manipulation of counterpoint is one of the greatest resources of composition. Hearing again some familiar passages of Bach and Vivaldi from this perspective affords the chance to experience, understand, and refine the principle of harmonic independence a little further.

SALIENCE OF DIVERGENT DIMENSIONS

If divergent dimensions of harmonic rhythm produce a certain kind of musical tension, it is reasonable to think that this tension increases, or at least becomes more present, with the perceptibility of the divergence. The more salient the divergence is, the more keenly felt the musical tension; the clearer the convergence, the more effective the resolution. Compare, for example, the beginning of Vivaldi's "Winter" Concerto (ex. 10-3) to the most motile measures in Bach's A Major Prelude (ex. 9-1, mm. 4–5). The Bach has a variety of speeds going on at once: the steady eighth notes in the textural, phenomenal, and first-level root dimensions; the slower second-level root; and the more irregular bass pitch and functional dimensions. By contrast, the Vivaldi has three very clearly differentiated speeds for the first six bars: the eighths of the texture, the whole notes of the phenomenal, and the very long, virtual immobility of the other dimensions. Now there is no doubt that the Bach passage seems faster and more active, owing to its comparatively rapid focal stream (dotted quarters, compared to whole notes in Vivaldi) and therefore conveys an excitement of forward propulsion. But the "Winter" Concerto has more of a completely different, nervous kind of tension—the tension of harmonic independence.

Ex. 10-2. Chorale "Herr Gott, Dich Loben Allen Wir," from the Genevan Psalter (1551).

Ex. 10-3. Vivaldi, Concerto op. 8, no. 4, "Winter," I, mm. 1–12.

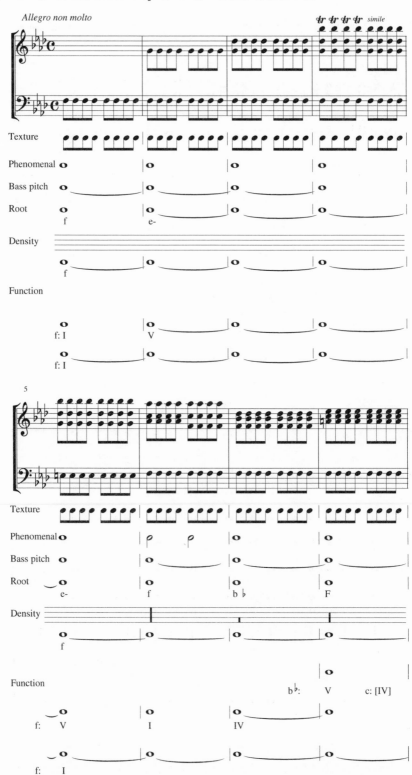

Ex. 10-3. *Continued*

This sensation derives from the very origins of counterpoint, which originally meant "note against note" (punctus contra punctum). In short, when important melodic notes change, chords should change too. That is part of common listening experience and is the experience of music history. Harmonizations like that of the hymn in example 10-2 seem normal, easy. But Vivaldi pits insistent attacks on every eighth note, amplified by phenomenal changes every eight attacks, against a triad that will not budge. The stubbornness of the implied E diminished triad, not to mention the more abstract F pedal, acts contrary to experience and expectation. The shivering eighth notes continually promise faster changes, but they do not come.

The comparison of these two passages implies that it is not the passage with a variety of divergence that creates the greatest tension of harmonic independence but the passage where the divergence seems most highly contrasted, most *stratified*.

What creates stratification? Perhaps the most important factor is the difference in speed between salient dimensions. How short are Vivaldi's eighths compared to the E diminished triad (1:32)! In the Bach passage the smallest ratio is 1:6, and for that we must invoke the most abstract functional rhythm.

A second factor is the degree of unanimity of the active dimensions on the different speeds. Bach's music certainly offers more variety of speeds among the dimensions, but it is precisely that variety that makes it harder to hear the contrast between the fastest and the slowest. Bach's divergence is carefully graded; Vivaldi's is starkly contrasted so that there is no missing it. The only stepping-stone between the textural rhythm and the root rhythm is the phenomenal, and that is already a perceptual leap: the phenomenal is eight times slower. Bach's passage is like that of a romantic watercolor where one hue blends subtly into another. By standing back one can see the color changes, of course, but their contrast is not highly articulated. Vivaldi's is more like a Cubist work where a few strident colors are butted one up against the other without any transition. The romantic technique can be very beautiful, but like the Bach it is calmer, isn't it?

Would the concerto be more exciting if Vivaldi had eliminated the phenomenal changes by starting out with the fully formed E diminished triad, thus contrasting the trembling eighth notes directly with the motionless root and function rhythms? Try it; the effect is dismal. Our attempt to maximize stratification fails because each of those eighth notes is a musical event that requires some kind of organization, patterning, to enable the human mind to comprehend it. Thirty-two iterations of the same diminished triad are simply too many for the perceiving mind to handle; a puzzled boredom quickly ensues. By building the triad measure by measure, Vivaldi breaks those thirty-two into four groups of eight, which not only is easier to process but also increases the harmonic tension on a completely different plane by continually adding dissonant intervals. Stratification has its limits.[3]

Stratification naturally calls to mind the idea of the bifocal stream (chapter 9) that splits the listener's attention between two speeds of harmonic motion. The presence of a bifocal stream may indeed contribute to the stratification of dimensions described here, but it is really a different attribute of the harmonic rhythm. A bifocal stream may arise, for instance, without a great difference in speeds between the two streams that it comprises. For a moment or two in measure 4 of the Bach, there is a bifocal stream, and the ratio of speeds is 3:1. This ratio is irrelevant to whether there is a bifocal stream or not. What matters is that there is competition for the listener's attention. To stratification, however, the ratio of the difference is most relevant, as Vivaldi has shown. There is no bifocal stream in the "Winter" Concerto, but the stratification gives the beginning an intensity that is as acute as in the Bach but feels quite different because its source is harmonic independence and not speed.

QUALITIES OF TENSIONS

In other words, the tension of harmonic independence has a quality different from that of speed, even though the sensation of each depends on the salience of particular harmonic dimensions. The focal stream produces a tension of pure speed, deriving from attention to one facet of the harmonic texture: how fast it is changing. This acceleration can change from moment to moment, of course, and so this tension is perceptually immediate and volatile. Harmonic divergence, by contrast, comes from a perception of the texture as a whole, its aggregate quality. It takes time to notice this disturbance, this failure of the various streams to match up as expected, the dragging of one motion against the surging of another. Such independence produces a more elastic kind of tension that begins unnoticed and grows tauter the longer it lasts. Thus tension can increase within a passage even when the divergence visible in the graph remains constant, as happens in Vivaldi's concerto. This is how the elasticity of harmonic independence differs most sharply from the immediate quality of speed. A focal stream of eighth notes does not become more tense as it goes, generally speaking, but a constant stream of eighth notes in one dimension against very sustained durations in another may well build to a climax.

Recall one of the hypotheses derived from harmonic speed: that, all things being equal, the abstract focal stream creates more tension than the superficial. Is there such an asymmetry in the tensions of harmonic independence?

The zero point of independence tension is complete convergence, which normally happens only at cadences. When divergence comes about, it is possible only in one direction: the slower dimensions are the more abstract, and they diverge from the faster ones at the surface. For that is the practicality of harmonic abstraction: it is a cognitive collection of faster events into a single organizing event. Harmonic embedding is a fine example: the triads creating a secondary dominant relation are abstracted into a single high-level function in the governing key, which must have longer duration—greater than or equal to their totality—in order to collect them. It is obviously impossible to have roots changing faster than phenomenal chords because no root can change without a phenomenal change. The bass pitch, true enough, is more independent and may remain stationary while roots and functions move, but that is rare. By and large, the dimensional graph, reading from top to bottom, proceeds from the surface to the abstract, from the faster to the slower motions. Divergence runs in one direction only. Surface dimensions cannot change more slowly than the abstract.

But composers occasionally create the illusion that they do. One source of this magic is pedal points.

Pedal points usually articulate high-level harmonic functions and they are explicit agents of embedding (chapter 7). From the point of view of musical texture, however, a pedal tone is simply a melody that has stopped moving while other melodies and harmonic events of all kinds continue around it. It is an explicit defiance of the historical conception of punctus contra punctum: when chords change, so must melodies, and vice versa. Because pedal points are surface events, they shout for attention, symbolizing stationary events that diverge from the harmonic rhythm, even though they are not technically part of harmonic rhythm; a pedal may not show up in the dimensional graph when it is drowned out by the other voices making textural rhythm. But because it is so outstanding in the texture, the pedal tone may create its own very acute and dynamic tension that arises from this illusion of harmonic divergence.

Try to imagine the Vivaldi (ex. 10-3) without the F pedal—say the bass moves to E_3 in measure 2. Harmonic tension immediately falls, owing to less dissonance, of course, but also because the stratification of the divergence is less; the high-level root and function graphs disappear completely. But most of all we miss the F's stubborn resistance to all those factors of the E-diminished triad.

Bach's pedal points in the opening bars of the A Major Prelude (ex. 9-1) interact with the harmonic rhythm so significantly that the music is unimaginable without them. Here they are not in the bass yet still build the more abstract harmonic dimensions. They create the vivid illusion of a texture that lags the harmonic rhythm because Bach establishes the fast root and function rhythms before the first pedal—the C-sharp$_5$—is ever heard. The divergence in the texture, imperceptible at first because it requires time to develop, becomes noticeable in measure 2 and intense in measure 3, when the first-level root and function dimensions accelerate to underscore the two divergent streams. At this moment Bach sounds his longest pedal of all. The elastic tension rapidly grows taut, and the move to the first subdominant harmony on the fourth beat is like the release of a great spring. The release into the varied activity of the next bar relaxes much of the tension of harmonic independence and converts it into pure speed, a most beautiful effect.

CONVERSION OF TENSIONS

Thinking about and listening to the tensions of harmonic rhythm teaches that the situation is almost never one of "on or off" but rather "this kind or that kind." This is true of musical tension in general.[4] In terms of harmonic divergence, measure 4 of the prelude (ex. 9-1) begins a relaxation, but in terms of harmonic speed, the abstract focal stream heightens the

excitement that soon drives toward a major harmonic event, the first modulation. Vivaldi, too, converts one kind of tension into another, although
less suddenly (ex. 10-3). After measure 6, changes in root and function make
divergence less salient, less acute, while increasing the pace of other harmonic events. Here it is not the durations in the graph but the multiplicity
of functional interpretations that gives the clue. The acceleration felt in
measures 7–11 owes much to the number of times the listener is forced to
reconsider, to rehear, what is recently past. By measure 10, divergence has
all but disappeared, and the harmonic rhythm is faster all around, preparing
the soloist's first brilliance.

Such conversions are at the heart of musical discourse. The handling of
musical tension—not just that of harmonic rhythm, but all kinds—is the
composer's chief means of creating and controlling musical effects and
structures. As an example of how harmonic rhythm participates in the
articulation of a complete form, consider a ritornello of Bach, from his
Mass in B Minor (ex. 10-4).

For a baroque composer such as Bach, the ritornello that introduces an
aria or chorus contains most of the musical elements to be heard in the
whole movement, including the opening and cadential gestures and all the
material needed for *Fortspinnung*, or working with the principal motives.
Because it is brief yet complete, the ritornello makes a good case study for
harmonic rhythm.

The aria begins with about the simplest spectrum of harmonic rhythm
that can be had with traditional harmony: textural and phenomenal rhythm
united, a moving bass, and a simple root progression yielding fairly straightforward functions. The degree of independence is low, homorhythmic motion high: most of the tension is in the speed of the changes and in the
harmonic functions themselves. The immediate embedding of a G major
center creates a momentary swell before the first cadence (m. 2) and hints
at future complications. These duly arrive in the fourth measure. Bach has
changed the bass line ever so slightly, and now its counterpoint with the
violins moves the focal stream to a slower, more abstract level of root
movement. At the same moment, the G major embedding from the beginning is recalled but now is set off the strong beats to bring a metric
tension into play. The long dominant and subdominant in the following
measures are similarly reinforced, and all these embedded functions sound
against the solid, long-held roots and functions. As this divergence grows
taut, the sixteenths in the violins are now relentless, intensifying the contrast with the slower, more complex textures below. The peak of complexity
arrives in measures 7 and 8, when both kinds of root motion accelerate
and pull against the prolonged subdominant lasting eight long beats. But
the concluding measure 9 is all dénouement: the slower dimensions, even
the most abstract functional level, catch up with the faster ones, quickly

Ex. 10-4. J. S. Bach, Christe Eleison from the *Mass in B Minor*, mm. 1–10.

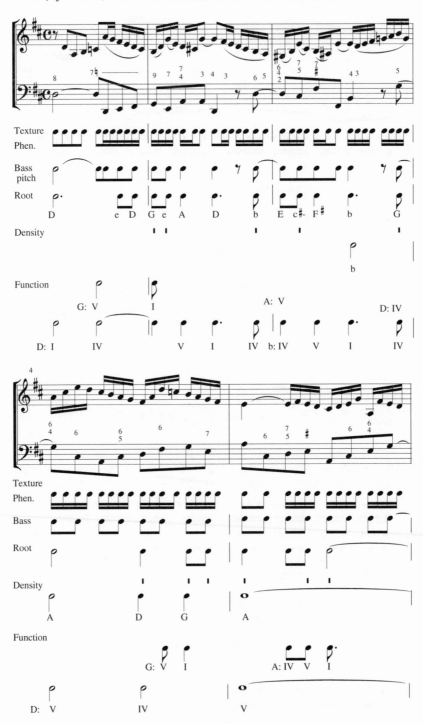

126

simplifying the rhythmic texture but making the speed of the harmonic rhythm more salient by joining the focal stream. Bach's counterpoint, by suddenly insisting on explicit roots and strong functions, converts the tension from the divergent kind to that of harmonic function, rounding off the ritornello in convincing and elegant simplicity without compromising in the least his driving violin melody.

Unified texture at the beginning, increasing harmonic divergence through the middle, a rapid conversion to speed tension for the cadence: this pattern appears repeatedly in traditional forms of functional harmony. Given the nature of the tensions of harmonic rhythm, it is quite a logical pattern. The tension of divergence cannot be created instantly. Neither can it be resolved precisely, since the listener needs time to perceive that dimensions are once more coincident. Its climactic effects fit best in the last third of the ritornello. Then there is plenty of time to prepare carefully the embedded functions and other divergences that build the peak. And where else for the unleashing of harmonic speed but at the end, where the virtue of pinpoint control can articulate the final resolution with greatest precision?

The conversion from divergence to speed is itself a special effect—particularly when accomplished rapidly, as in this piece—that creates a memorable moment. But that is merely one of the marvels of a beautifully coordinated harmonic rhythm. It is nearly impossible to convey the technical achievement of Bach's counterpoint in this construction, the degree of superb coordination of so many disparate elements of his music. He must not only control the speeds of the various dimensions through the handling of just two contrapuntal voices, but also the order of the functions they produce. It is not enough, for example, to slow the abstract functions in measures 5–8 and then speed them up in 8 and 9: they must be the right harmonic functions in the right sequence. The greatest wonder is that he can do all this without the slightest discontinuity in the two melodies, textbook models of rhythmic and motivic consistency, to say nothing of melodic grace.

CHAPTER II.

RHYTHMS OF NON-FUNCTIONAL

HARMONY

*T*HE HARMONY of musical languages prevalent in the twentieth century, most of the Renaissance, the Middle Ages, and non-Western traditions is likely to be non-functional. "Non-functional" is a somewhat catchall term that covers music whose stable chords either are not triads at all or, if they are, do not have the syntactic relations of tonic, dominant, and subdominant that we hear in Bach, Mozart, and Chopin. Listeners therefore do not sense one chord leading to another in the same way as with the functional languages of the "common practice" period that concerned Walter Piston in his *Harmony*. Listeners may be entirely unable to predict the next harmonic event in a progression or have little in the way of expectation about it. If they can predict, they predict according to different rules of syntax.

The complete dimensional graph of Guillaume de Machaut's first movement from his *Messe de Notre Dame* (ex. 11-1), composed about 1350, looks impoverished compared with most of the music considered thus far.[1] The additional density graph for the phenomenal harmonic rhythm is more than offset by the missing functional and bass pitch dimensions. There is only one level of root rhythm.

Fewer dimensions is a logical consequence of non-functional harmony. No non-functional musical language can have dimensions of function, by definition. And since there are no functions for it to symbolize, the bass voice of Machaut's non-functional polyphony loses the special role it has in functional music; the bass is simply a voice in the texture like any other, and the bass pitch dimension disappears.

Ex. 11-1. Machaut, Kyrie I from *La Messe de Notre Dame*.

There are fewer dimensions in comparison with a functional graph, and the meanings of the remaining ones change. One might suspect, quite reasonably, that when harmonic texture becomes so spare, there is no need to graph; perusal of the score itself suffices. But the graph, remember, is simply a means to understand what is going on; perusers sufficiently talented to do without must still resort to the principles of interpretation—speed and independence—that give any image of harmonic rhythm, graphic or imaginary, its meaning.

In terms of dimensional theory, a non-functional musical language has fewer resources of harmonic rhythm than functional music has. In this sense it seems impoverished. There are fewer dimensions with which to create tensions and resolutions of harmonic independence, so those dimensions that remain may create less salience in the harmonic motions, attract-

Ex. 11-1. *Continued*

ing less attention and producing less effect. Now this is no wholesale in-
dictment of non-functional languages, because, like all languages, they make
syntactic compensations.[2] If the harmonic aspect is less powerful, the contrapuntal, or the purely melodic or rhythmic, may be more. And however
attenuated it may be in general, the power of harmonic rhythm in particular instances nevertheless contributes remarkable effects of coherence, articulation, and expression to the music. In fact, because in general the
harmony of non-functional music has received comparatively little attention, particularly in music composed before 1600, the analysis of these effects is wide open.

But to make cogent dimensional analyses of non-functional music, the
particular syntax of the non-functional musical language under discussion

must shape the analysis. If triads are not stable chords in medieval polyphony, what should take their place? When Debussy writes parallel chords to
make his "triad melodies," what is the effect on the sense of high-level
roots? In other words, the historical and linguistic context of the music
must inform the dimensional technique in each case. In the end, the dimensional graph may well communicate different kinds of information than
one for Bach or Chopin because the individual dimensions may mean subtly
different things, even though they share the same names. The analytical
issues that arise with all the variety of non-functional musical languages of
course, cannot be completely catalogued in a single chapter, but the three
analyses that follow may give some idea of the kinds of questions one
should ask.

MEDIEVAL POLYPHONY: MACHAUT (C. 1350)

In Machaut's four-voice polyphony, stable chords are built of the only two
intervals known in medieval theory to be "perfect consonances": perfect
octaves and perfect fifths above the lowest sounding pitch. Triads do occur
with frequency, but because they must include the "imperfect consonance"
of the third, they are not sufficiently stable to conclude a cadence. The
dimension of root rhythm for Machaut's music, therefore, records the
changes in "open fifth" chord structures only. Since no third factors can
alter the quality and the syntax allows no fifths but perfect ones, there is
no quality dimension at all. The letters, all capital, beneath the duration
symbols in the root dimension denote the lower pitch of the open fifth or
octave dyad.[3]

This change in the meaning of the root dimension is reflected in its
density graph. Only two factors are possible in an open fifth chord; anach-
ronistic third factors do not contribute to the density. So the first chord of
the piece (D_3-A_3-D_4-A_4) has a density of four because the pitch-class A is
the perfect fifth above pitch-class D: all four voices contribute. But the G_3
in the tenor of the third chord is not part of the E-B open fifth dyad: the
density is three. But there is no need to worry about factors in the density
graph beneath the phenomenal harmonic rhythm. The phenomenal harmony, remember, does not distinguish between syntactic and nonsyntactic
chord structures: a new pitch in a voice is all that is required, and that is
why the phenomenal density of the third chord is four. This graph, by its
own definition, must record densities equal to or higher than the density
graph of the root rhythm.

So much for adapting the dimensional technique to Machaut's musical
language. Once the graph is done, what can it tell us about his music?

Machaut uses harmonic rhythm to establish and control the meter of his composition. Meter in the sacred music of the Middle Ages and Renaissance is a most subtle and delicate aspect of rhythm. It rarely loses the essential distinction of strong and weak beats, but in general that distinction is not very great. In other words, the strong beats have only slightly more weight than the weak beats, in comparison with, say, dance music or most music of the baroque and classical periods, where the difference is marked with a heavy hand and there is seldom any doubt about which is the strong beat.[4] In this piece by Machaut, the higher-level meter of six-beat groups (six half notes in this transcription) is quite clear throughout, but its subdivision into groups of three or two is often chimerical, sounding as if it changes from one bar to the next. This is what gives this sacred piece its characteristically effortless flow, an almost chantlike quality that, naturally, brings along important semantic associations with the Gregorian tradition.

How does harmonic rhythm contribute to this complex sense of meter? In general, harmonic rhythm can establish and sustain a metric pattern because it entails changes of harmony. Every change makes a perceivable event, a moment of time that is accented by the change. By consistently selecting certain changes for special emphasis, Machaut uses harmony to create the regular pattern defining the high-level, six-beat group; at the same time, by varying the emphasis and timing of changes within that group, he creates an unpredictable flow within.

The main influence on Machaut's meter is the root rhythm. One can easily read in that graph how the first chord of each six-beat group (here, each notated measure) is longer than its neighbor chords.[5] In five of the first seven measures, the first chord occupies fully half the measure, and in the other two bars, one-third. It is a renowned principle of meter that a longer event has greater perceptual weight than a shorter one, all other things being equal. This is the agogic accent. Machaut applies this principle by sounding his longest root durations at the beginnings of six-beat groups.

This handling of the root rhythm is supported and ratified by his handling of the counterpoint, which shows up in the density graph beneath. Through the first ten bars, every first beat coincides with a chord having a density of four, the highest possible, except measure 6, while the great majority of other beats have much lower densities. Machaut will not let us miss his weightiest chord changes. The choice of chord, too, matters to the sense of meter, even if it is not, strictly speaking, germane to harmonic rhythm. Five of the first nine downbeat chords are D chords, and so tie the stability of Machaut's tonic to its traditional location on the stable strong beat.

Within the six-beat groups the distinction of strong and weak is much less consistent and clear. In the first bar, for example, the root rhythm would suggest two subgroups of triple (two 3/2 bars). But the E chord is accented by its higher density and by the high B_4 in the triplum voice, which support a perception of three subgroups of duple (three 2/2 bars). Such conflicts characterize the whole piece, with no two successive measures the same. Density patterns and root duration patterns constantly vary, sometimes encouraging the 3/2 perception, at other times the 2/2 perception, always with equivocation and compromise. Thus the overall organizing power and stability of the six-beat group never stifles the mystical ebb and flow of the interior (lower-level) meters.

At the midpoint of the piece the graph indicates more equivocation even on the higher level. In measures 8 and 10 the second chord, not the first, is the longest, creating a more pronounced syncopation. Other beats become more active in the counterpoint; high densities occur more unpredictably. After the downbeat of measure 11, low densities abound, and the root durations are long, more metrically ambiguous. All this is part of Machaut's design for the climax of this short movement near the end. Having established the meter for seven measures, he can depend on listeners maintaining that pattern in perception and thus can afford to gamble with more liberally weighted offbeats. Then, at the moment when our metric security threatens to break down, he restores it and quickly drives to the cadence (mm. 13–14).

This climax depends in part on another aspect of harmonic rhythm: independence. Even though there are only two different dimensions of duration, the textural/phenomenal and the root, Machaut exploits their coordination to shape the composition. The pattern is simple: convergence to divergence to convergence to greater divergence to final convergence. The first three bars set this pattern for the whole piece: the first with its maximal convergence, the second with significant divergence, the third with relatively high convergence between the two dimensions. From this point harmonic independence increases until measure 8, when a curious articulation occurs. Here is the fastest motion of the whole movement, harmonically speaking, yet the texture is paradoxically relaxed because of the sudden high convergence Machaut imposes on his counterpoint. It is a classic case of conversion of one kind of tension into another, almost as if he were preparing for the end. But the two dimensions diverge gradually in measure 10, and then follows the most extremely independent writing of all, with the longest continuous string of quarter-note articulations pulling against the suddenly slower root motions. This tension coordinates with the meter already described, and both resolve conclusively toward the end of the penultimate measure.

Harmonic rhythm may contribute to the end in one more way, revealed by the upper density graph, which is another adaptation to Machaut's musical language. With so few active dimensions, the relative salience of each may be quite different from that in a functional graph, and it seems wise to analyze each as fully as possible. At first the comparison appears to make no difference; there are remarkably few places where Machaut makes a strong phenomenal change without a new root, until the last five bars, that is. Supporting and amplifying the other harmonic tensions, Machaut suddenly creates a series of high-density phenomenal changes. The effect is to highlight the phenomenal harmonic rhythm, of course, and perhaps to create in our perception a bifocal stream, particularly in measures 11 and 12, for the first and only time in the piece. The salience of this effect will depend a lot on the performance of that syncopated triplum melody. If those offbeat quarter notes cut through sharply, perceiving the bifocal stream is easy, and the tension is greatest as the music approaches the end.

The traditional approach to rhythm in Machaut and music of his time is to analyze the isorhythm—the recurring patterns of pitch and duration in the tenor voice. In this Kyrie, Machaut fashions his tenor part on a traditional Kyrie chant melody and gives it a durational pattern (talea) that recurs every two measures (♩ . ♩ ♩ ♩ . ♩). (The melodic pattern, or *color*, does not begin to repeat until the next movement of the mass.)[6] However, the movement is actually doubly isorhythmic, for the lowest voice, the *contratenor*, also presents a much longer durational pattern lasting six measures. It is a most curious instance, for Machaut does not end the piece after twelve bars, which would have accomodated both patterns evenly (tenor: six times a two-measure pattern; contratenor: two times a six-measure pattern). Rather he composes an extension of two bars that allows the tenor talea a seventh complete repetition and the lower contratenor a nearly coincident motion (mm. 13–14).

The key moments in double isorhythm are those of coincidence—in this piece at measures 7 and 13—when the two patterns finish up together and begin anew. In the first case, harmonic rhythm contributes to the clarity of this moment, for the root rhythm is the slowest of any measure in the composition and even the phenomenal is little faster, as if Machaut wished to articulate harmonically his principal contrapuntal device. To do so next time around (m. 13), however, would be to make an anticlimax of Machaut's extension. He does not relinquish the divergence of the harmonic streams until the extension is nearly over.

RENAISSANCE POLYPHONY:
DUFAY (C. 1450)

The Renaissance musical language of Guillaume Dufay provides triads as stable chord structures in its syntax. Open octaves and fifths still occur but much more rarely, usually being reserved for the very first and last chords of a movement. Dufay's triads do not have functional relations among themselves, however, so his language is certainly non-functional. But major and minor triads may qualify as points of resolution in harmonic progression, and the dimensional graph must accommodate their movement (ex. 11-2).

This accommodation alters the root graph vis-à-vis Machaut in two ways. First, it becomes again a root/quality graph. But the quality rarely changes from major to minor, as we hear often in more recent music; rather the quality changes, from an open chord to a triad, or vice versa, as happens in the first two measures of the Kyrie: the initial C chord consists entirely of pitches from the C pitch-class, an open sound, which then passes to a major triad in measure 2. Second, the addition of a chord factor, the third factor, to the harmonic syntax makes it much easier to sketch multiple levels of root change. In this Kyrie such bilevel progression is never sustained for long, but its occasional rhythmic complications are substantial.

Dufay's Kyrie is significantly longer than Machaut's, which means that it depends more on an explicitly articulated structure that listeners can hear and use to help them organize this complex polyphony in their perception. This is exactly the principal role of harmonic rhythm for Dufay. It helps him articulate the cadences.

The first major articulation of the movement is actually a set of three closely grouped and similar cadences: the Landini formula that finishes in measure 7, a variant into measure 9, and a longer, more elaborate gesture that concludes in measure 13, where it overlaps with the second phrase of the cantus firmus (tenor voice) beginning the next section. Once again the sense of meter makes these gestures stand out.

As in the Machaut, meter is a fluid affair, but Dufay's deployment of it involves a quite different strategy. He is little concerned with establishing an unmistakable sense of meter from the outset. He merely suggests a gentle triple meter by the motion in the cantus melody and by the three root and quality changes, one per bar, on the higher level. Then syncopations set in immediately; Dufay obviously has great faith in his listeners' maintaining this spiritual sort of meter on their own for a time, since it finds little support in measures 4 through 6. Suddenly, then, the root changes begin to behave themselves. The longer ones stress the downbeats consistently, bringing out each cadential gesture as a resolution, until one last syncopation—the long C chord in measures 11 and 12—supplies enough tension to carry the music to the cadence in 13.

The density graph shows how Dufay's counterpoint underscores these important root changes that define the meter. At first there is no coordination of high density with downbeats, but at the crucial moments around those cadences there is every coordination.

Ex. 11-2. Dufay, Kyrie I from *Missa Se La Face Ay Pale.*

The focal stream, which resides almost entirely in the higher-level root rhythm, also helps to shape the first large phrase around the cadences, particularly the last. Here the motion is the fastest of the piece so far (mm. 10–11); then it brakes into a broad syncopation that reduces the speed tension as the cadential gesture plays out. This precise moment (m. 12), where

Ex. 11-2. *Continued*

Dufay's voice leading is most angular, offers the best possibility for a bifocal stream in the root rhythm, whose tension resolves with the downbeat of the cadential bar.

In similar fashion, Dufay coordinates the dimensions of harmonic rhythm for the other cadences articulating the piece, even to the point of

Ex. 11-2. *Continued*

distinguishing their respective strengths. The second cadence on D in measure 21 sounds like an abbreviated version of the first one. Again there is
a hint of harmonic independence immediately preceding, again a bit of
harmonic syncopation in measure 19, a touch of metric dissonance before
the security of strong downbeats. But here the speed of harmonic rhythm
is the principal shaper of the cadential gesture: the sudden acceleration in
measure 20 followed by the longest harmony since the beginning leaves

Ex. 11-2. *Continued*

no doubt of the articulation. Only the overlapping of the cantus firmus (highest voice here) carries the motion onward.

The next strong cadence does not occur until the end, leaving in between an extraordinary amount of music for a single phrase. To throw the listener a provisional anchor at least, Dufay fashions a kind of medial cadence, a weak articulation in measure 29. Along with the downward course of the top melody, density and harmonic independence reduce the tension just slightly, right in the middle of a cantus firmus phrase, to make the breathing space before the final run.[7] Then, like Machaut, Dufay appears to throw caution to the wind. The last seven measures have root durations and densities that discourage any consistent perception of meter. Measures 32–35 scan more easily in duple, with a giant hemiola typically placed before the final cadence. The last high-density articulation falls on the downbeat of measure 35, after which the listener must float weightless to the final chord. The new level of root motion charges this moment with the tension of a bifocal stream. When convergence arrives at last, it is too sudden to absorb all the forward momentum, so Dufay's plagal cadence gracefully delays the final moment.

Because Dufay's musical language has few highly defined cadential formulas, he must define them himself. In this movement he follows the classic strategy of setting the terms with unmistakable clarity on first occurrence, attenuating the profile for the medial gestures of the piece, and returning with full force for the end. Harmonic rhythm is one of the essential ingredients of this cadential technique.

TWENTIETH-CENTURY
IMPRESSIONISM: DEBUSSY (1910)

Dufay's harmony is non-functional because the musical communities that preceded him never developed those syntactic relations for triads. He was never aware that the harmony of his music was "non-functional," for the concept had no meaning for him. In both an epistemological and practical sense, the dichotomy of functional versus non-functional harmony did not exist. For Claude Debussy, however, composing in the decades around the turn of the twentieth century, it certainly did exist. His music is to a great extent a revolution against a functional system that ceased to inspire his creative powers. But, like most successful revolutions, his never cut off the past entirely but rather reached an accommodation with it while inventing an essentially new musical language. To be sure, there are entire passages of his music without a single conventional triad, but many others make explicit use of them, even if functional syntax is denied them. Debussy occupies a far different historical position than does Dufay, for he knows that the musical community for which he composes will recognize triads, bass lines, and other vestiges of conventional grammar and bring with that recognition a multiplicity of associations and expectations. These Debussy can exploit.

To account for such nuances, which are very much a part of the essence of Debussy's music, the analyst must exercise judgment, almost a vigilance on the role of harmonic features. Is the bass line just another voice, or does it "carry the harmony" in some obscure fashion? Are triads linked by function or just voice-leading?

The first four bars of Debussy's "Des Pas Sur La Neige" direct attention to the phenomenal dimension of harmonic rhythm, for there is virtually nothing else going on (ex. 11-3). The lower-level roots are discontinuous and the abstract D triad immobile. The texture is actually much plainer, rhythmically, than it looks in the graph. If grace notes were substituted for Debussy's fussy notation, we would see a high degree of convergence at the beginning in all dimensions. The opening effect is one of nearly total stillness.

What does it mean when all attention is on the phenomenal harmonic rhythm? It means that there is almost no sense of any harmonic rhythm at all. One aspect of harmonic rhythm that the dimensional graphing technique cannot capture explicitly is the fact that the different kinds of harmonic rhythm have different weights or perceptual salience. When triads

Ex. 11-3. Debussy, "Des Pas Sur La Neige," from *Preludes*, vol. 1, mm. 1–15.

move, the listener knows from long experience that a multiplicity of melodies is moving, too. One logically implies the other. But a phenomenal rhythm can be effected by a single melody against a constant harmonic ground, as it is here. In this sense the activity of the notation overstates the perception. The analyst's interpretation must compensate.[8]

Ex. 11-3. *Continued*

The other harmonic features are not without purpose here. The abstract D chord arising from the ostinato never really moves, except by disappearing entirely in measure 5, but it forms a center of gravity against which the melody weakly tries to escape. It also provides a standard of reference. When the melody blends into it with the consonance of the first complete D triad, the gesture completes the first short phrase (m. 4).

Harmony explodes into action, relatively speaking, with the onset of the parallel triads in measure 5. The abrupt shift of the focal stream means a

Ex. 11-3. *Continued*

slight lessening of speed tension, but that is more than compensated for by the sheer novel weight of explicit harmonic movement. Such clarity is short-lived. A bit of recitative in the right hand (mm. 6–7) reintroduces the ephemeral harmony of the beginning. New motion in the bass wrests the focal stream from the roots, whose identities are increasingly obscure but are, in a typical Debussy touch, clarified by the bass itself on the weak beats. The root motion briefly amplifies this faster motion in measure 10 before coming to rest on a G-flat/D-flat complex under the ostinato (m. 11). The bass then presents the fastest motion of the piece, pulling against the sustained chord in willful independence before subsiding, in measure 14, into an inversion of the original texture.

This long phrase (mm. 1–15) is an arch that trades sure but slow speed in the center against a gentle, phantomlike but faster movement at beginning and end. The beauty of the design owes something of its strangeness to the reversal of the normal course of events. Extremes of harmonic independence are supposed to power the middle of the phrase, and the convergence of dimensions finishes it. Debussy's successful *bouleversement* depends on his risking everything on the phenomenal harmonic rhythm, the motion that feels like gossamer even when it flies, and on his confidence that modern listeners, longing for triads, will grasp them in eagerly whenever they surface.

The second long phrase (mm. 16–25, not quoted here) accelerates this arch pattern by introducing a bass line under the ostinato almost immediately. The sense of harmonic speed is therefore stronger but also slower, since the focal stream no longer occupies the phenomenal dimension. When the parallel chords return, Debussy extends their texture while at the same time denaturing them so that they are no longer recognizable triads. The dissolution to the phenomenal that we heard at the end of the first phrase just barely occurs in the second, as the slow bass line quits only three beats before the end. The second phrase, surely modeled on the textural procedures of the first, actually expands the middle active part at the expense of the phenomenally centered parts—quite logical for the middle of the composition.

The last long phrase (ex. 11-4) begins immediately with the parallel chord texture, yet because the convergence is suddenly so high compared to the immediately preceding activity, this recapitulation has nearly the calm desolation of the opening. Added tones begin to obscure the sense of triad identity, and therefore harmonic rhythm, almost immediately, as if Debussy were rushing toward a final dissolution that will end the piece. Then, just after the onset of the recitativelike melody that has always accompanied just such an effect, it is transfigured by a sudden upwelling of sixth chords, coinciding with Debussy's most emotional advisory in the score ("like a tender and sad regret"). It is the most explicit convergence of the phenomenal with the deeper levels of harmonic rhythm and the fastest aggregate harmonic rhythm of the composition.

The climax is touchingly brief; the two dimensions diverge again but slowly, perhaps, to use Debussy's image, regretfully. The return of the ostinato brings a jarring return to the tonic, which accelerates the dissolution of the texture that we know must come, that the train of triads already began. This is a truer recollection of the beginning, with its fleeting perceptions of discontinuous triads. Again the focal stream returns to the phantom phenomenal level, never again to leave. The upper voices achieve their melodic goals before the lower, and Debussy ends the piece with a kind of plagal cadence. But its purpose here is different from one by Dufay, which must allow the convergence of voices already present. With his arpeggiation of a G dyad, Debussy actually increases harmonic independence for a moment. His purpose instead is to complete the texture, to bring back all the harmonic elements—root and bass as well as phenomenal—that have shaped the composition. In a non-functional language, final resolution depends on such subtle details.

It could be that, for Debussy, the primary function of harmonic rhythm is not the creation of musical tension, for, in this prelude at least, the fastest speeds and most extreme divergences are in fact quite restrained. It may be instead the definition of textures, as in this last cadence, that articulate not just the active and restful moments but the form of the piece. In that case, interpreting the dimensional graph leans away from a continuously dynamic picture of listening and toward a synchronic series of rhythmic images, profiles, or fingerprints. "Des Pas Sur La Neige" establishes a pattern of textures in its opening fifteen bars that employs the tensions of

Ex. 11-4. Debussy, "Des Pas Sur La Neige," from *Preludes*, vol. 1, mm. 26–36.

Ex. 11-4. *Continued*

harmonic rhythm obversely, allowing the ephemeral phenomenal dimension to make the greatest speed, contrasting that with a stodgier but more salient root and bass rhythm. Such cross-purposes rein in the forward motion of the music. There is stillness and above all, a unique sequence of textures. Debussy wants us to hear not the movement but the moment and to allow each its individual impression.

CHAPTER 12.

FIVE CRITICAL QUESTIONS

*A*T THIS point the dimensional theory of harmonic rhythm is complete as far as I have taken it. Refinements are no doubt possible and desirable. But however much it may be improved, it would rarely be employed as the sole means to answer a question of music analysis or to tackle an interesting problem in criticism. As a perspective on harmony, perhaps the most technically sophisticated element of the Western tradition, any means of understanding harmonic rhythm might put claim to some centrality, but at the same time it treats only one aspect of one element of a most complex and subtle art. What remains to be done here is to observe the technique in its proper role, that is, as a participant in music criticism, as a tool of analysis. Why does the community of Chopin lovers sense the climax of his A-flat Major Etude around measures 34–36? How can Debussy combine functional and non-functional triadic harmony in his first prelude? Why should a composer as contrapuntally accomplished as Josquin restrict himself to "melodies" of one pitch? What justifies the first fortissimo in Mozart's overture to *The Marriage of Figaro*? How do we sense harmonic movement in Bach's solo violin writing?

None of these questions about the musical experience of five famous and diverse works explicitly invokes harmonic rhythm. Indeed, dimensional analysis may have nothing to say about certain matters, since no method can answer everything. But if harmonic rhythm is an essential aspect of the Western tradition in general, a good analytical technique should have the power to partially explain the musical experience of that tradition. This

Ex. 12-1. Chopin, Etude op. 25, no. 1, in A-flat Major, mm. 1–36.

final chapter, then, addresses these five questions as an illustration of how this might be done. It provides some idea of the reach of harmonic rhythm.

CHOPIN: ETUDE OP. 25, NO. 1, IN A-FLAT MAJOR

The Chopin etude whose harmonic rhythm has been discussed from time to time (ex. 12-1) is a superb example of the romantic ideal of endless melody. The first authentic cadence of any weight does not occur until measure 36, and in fact it is the only one of importance in the high-level structure of the piece. Nothing except plagal reiterations follow it until the very last cadence at the end.

Traditional harmony gives a pretty good account of how Chopin man-

Ex. 12-1. *Continued*

ages to delay such an important harmonic articulation. The first eight bars lay out a luxurious antecedent phrase, but the dominant arrives so late that we barely have time to recognize it before Chopin has begun anew. Because of his explicit quotation of the opening material in bars 9 and 10 and because of his clear melodic subgrouping (4 bars plus 4 bars), the eight-bar phrasing pattern is unmistakable and the tonic harmony of bar 9 must be heard as a new beginning, never as resolution. The harmonic goal of the consequent is chromatically deflected to a cadence on C in measure 16, preserving the period exactly to form without letting the melody really finish.

Next follows a seemingly effortless but actually quite radical tour through a number of foreign tonal centers, finally arriving at the distant key of A major (m. 24). Now Chopin's masterly exploitation of piano register conjures an almost magical reorientation when, after a virtuoso chro-

Ex. 12-1. *Continued*

matic twist (m. 25), he sounds a D-flat₃ deep in the bass, instantly recalling the subdominant functions linked to that same sound in measures 5 and 13. A secure A-flat tonality restored, he moves immediately to the longest dominant function of the composition thus far, only to deflect its resolution with a deceptive cadence (m. 29). The last dominant function outstrips its predecessor by far and, again with exuberant play on the extreme register of the piano, arrives at the long-awaited tonic in a great harmonic and melodic climax.

Even in this conventional harmonic view, time is an indispensable accomplice. Yes, the identity of keys and triads functioning in them is critical to understanding this music, but so is their duration, their occurrence in the metric scheme, and their position in the phrase. What does a more nuanced account of harmonic rhythm have to add?

The placid consistency of the opening phrase covers a dynamic in the harmonic rhythm that joins with the harmonic functions to articulate its

Ex. 12-1. *Continued*

antecedent form. Beginning with virtually no motion at all except at the surface of the texture, Chopin slowly increases the speed and then the independence of the harmonic rhythm. The peak of tension falls in the second half, when the focal stream moves at quarter-note speed before shifting to the more abstract root movement by measure 7. This helps to brake the action, while the harmonic embedding clears just in time to provide some convergence in measure 8. The phrase articulation arises from a pattern of increasing speed shifting to increasing independence and slower speed, ending in a relative convergence.

This pattern is writ large through all the time remaining up to Chopin's climax. The false consequent phrase (mm. 9–16) begins exactly as the antecedent and so projects the same harmonic rhythm. But the parallel motion to C major is strangely calm. Where is the acceleration and intensification of texture experienced in the earlier phrase? For the moment, Chopin relies mostly on the tension of harmonic distance, saving increased harmonic speed to accompany his ever bolder harmonic reaches (mm. 17–23).

Ex. 12-1. *Continued*

Even here it is highly controlled—restrained in the consuming romantic quest for greater delay. The focal stream is abstract and slow through measure 19, but the rising fourth in the principal melody, first to F_5, then to A-flat$_5$ (mm. 18, 20), accompanies harmonic rhythm of ever-growing salience in the inner parts until its quarter-note speed infects the functional dimension in measure 21. Now high-density changes assault the listener faster as the focal stream takes on syncopations that pull against the slower root rhythm, which by measure 22 merely represents Chopin's ephemeral tonal centers. So weak and insecure are they that there is no higher-level functional dimension. The music here is full of speed and the harmonic exoticism of distance from A-flat.

Then as the melody climbs to heights it has not touched since near the beginning, Chopin's D-flat harmony brakes the harmonic rhythm with shocking abruptness and converts the former momentum into a tension arising from a multiplicity of functional implications (m. 26). Long durations briefly calm the storm; it is a false lull. Following the deceptive cadence

Ex. 12-1. *Continued*

(m. 29), the longest dominant accompanies a texture of intense stratification, which is finally compounded by harmonic embedding that both maximizes the independence and simultaneously drives the climax with the fastest harmonic rhythm that Chopin has used in the composition.

Dimensional analysis shows how the moments leading up to the cadence in measure 36 build the greatest tension of the etude on Chopin's brilliant coordination of harmonic function and harmonic rhythm, but that is but one part of the lesson harmonic rhythm can teach here. Whether this tension is "the greatest" of the piece is perhaps not the most interesting point. (After all, we knew that, and had a partial explanation for it already, didn't we?)

It would be a shame, for instance, to miss the graphic similarity of measures 33–36 to measures 6–8, for this implies a revised view of the antecedent-consequent pattern. Yes, Chopin begins with a textbook eight-

Ex. 12-1. *Continued*

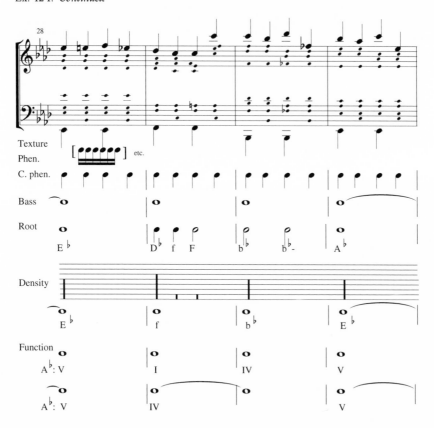

measure antecedent, but he answers with a tremendously extended, elaborated, and fantastic consequent that cannot match up with its mate and cadence properly until it completes a parallel rhythmic shape and texture, however titanic the proportions have now become. The fascination of this second "phrase" lies not so much in a steady crescendo of musical tension, rather like watching a missile ascend, but in the interplay of the various *kinds* of musical tension that Chopin draws from his palette. The typical metaphors for states of tension—"calm," "intensified," and so on—are inadequate to the richness, since they imply but a single dimension of rising and falling.

It would be a shame, too, to miss the dexterity of Chopin's inner part writing. An unfortunate consequence of his notation is that it is too easy to regard the etude as a two-voice composition accompanied by sonorous filler. But if we take only a single instance, measures 31 and 32, the significance of the little notes becomes clear. The bass is locked onto its long dominant, and the principal melody plays out an innocent chromatic se-

Ex. 12-1. *Continued*

quence. But the second leg of the sequence explodes into harmonic activity in the root rhythm that eventually leads the third leg to break its intended pattern and scale the high register in a histrionic ascent. Here the dimensional graph perhaps overstates the matter, because this is an explosion we barely notice until its effects are too great to ignore. The sheer consistency of the melodic sequence diverts all attention from the inner workings, yet how crucial they are. And how crucial are the details of Chopin's voice-leading, his choice of the exact pitches needed to convey the multiplicity of changes in the functional dimension that make this moment such an intense experience.

JOSQUIN: MOTET: "MISERERE MEI, DEUS" (TERTIA PARS)

How does a composer create a harmonic climax by contrapuntal, not functional, means? In other words, how are the tensions and resolutions of individual melodies, as opposed to those of dominant and tonic chords, brought to bear on a single moment in order to sculpt an essentially musical form? An impossibly large question, to be sure, but one to which harmonic rhythm may advance some response. The opening section of the third *pars* of Josquin's monumental motet offers some possibilities (ex. 12-2).

The monotone in all four voices is striking, not only in terms of the whole motet or even of Josquin's oeuvre but also in terms of the contrapuntal art of the high Renaissance. In a language of such harmonic and rhythmic constraint, melodic contour is a precious resource, one that Josquin, a consummate master of counterpoint, momentarily abandons. There are semantic reasons for this, certainly.[1] The text of the motet is Psalm 51, set in its considerable entirety. The ancient chant tradition that was Josquin's musical and spiritual heritage grounding most of his sacred composition prescribed that psalms were to be sung to a formulaic reciting tone. Unlike texts for hymns, mass ordinaries, and the innumerable propers, Psalm 51 has no traditional melody. Nevertheless, Josquin composes the entire motet around a cantus firmus, invented by him, that recalls this tradition: a monotone on the words "Miserere mei, Deus" (Have mercy on me, O God) with a single inflection upward on the penultimate syllable. (An instance appears in ex. 12-2, mm. 7–9, in the tenor.) Now, after the two great long essays on this conception that are the first two *partes* of this motet, Josquin allows the recitation psalm music to characterize all the other four voices. It sounds like a mystical, polyphonic psalm of ancient profundity.

But this singular texture does not last for long. The uppermost cantus voice breaks out with an inflection quite reminiscent of a psalm's cadential formula (m. 6), and the other voices immediately follow. After the contemplative beginning, the onset of the refrain and the entrance of the fifth voice with the *cantus firmus* in measure 7 bring on a remarkable intensification, a rapid and true climax of counterpoint that just as rapidly subsides into the traditional suspension cadence on C. So perhaps there are syntactic reasons, too, for the monotone.

It is much more than a simple matter of contrast. The monotone allows Josquin, by exploiting the very audible differences between the "open-fifth" and triadic sonorities, to imply almost from the outset two levels of root rhythm, the faster one responding to quality, the slower to pitch. It is a

Ex. 12-2. Josquin, Motet "Miserere mei, Deus," tertia pars, mm. 1–9.

Ex. 12-2. *Continued*

risky strategy; the chords change at nearly minimalist pace. Density remains at the absolute lowest. Can entrancement be far off? Happily, there is another harmonic aspect to hear. The polyphony of monotones creates an independent phenomenal harmonic rhythm, and that is where the focal stream begins.

All the dimensions maintain a kaleidoscopic independence until measure 4, when there is a sudden convergence in all but the textural rhythm, coinciding roughly with the new text phrase "et os meum." The momentary coincidence transfers the focal stream to the first root level, which now assumes the same speed as had the phenomenal at the beginning. This subtle transfer intensifies the texture, since the focal stream is now slightly more abstract and the weight of moving roots is greater than of single pitch changes. As the aggregate harmonic rhythm accelerates, densities rise, bringing the texture out of the mist in time to articulate a curious medial suspension cadence on C in measure 7. Its effect is felt and immediately annulled as the fifth voice makes its entrance.

Ex. 12-3. Josquin, Motet "Miserere mei, Deus," tertia pars, mm. 63–68.

The real cadence of this section occurs with the cadence of the cantus firmus, as it has for sixteen times now throughout the motet. Here Josquin creates a true wonder of Renaissance counterpoint: a third level of root movement. His imitative deployment of the scalar motive is so finely calculated that we cannot ignore the overall tonal center on C made so clear from the beginning, the continuity of the root motions coming out of the provisional cadence, or the additionally embedded quarter-note roots implied by a string of parallel sixth chords. This last divides the focal stream and buttresses the stratification of the texture at one stroke, a richly intensified harmonic texture of moving melodies. So answers Josquin the question of contrapuntal climax.

The convergence on the C cadence (m. 9) is both complete and sudden, prepared only by slight retardations in the faster dimensions. Thus the movement retains latent energy to begin the next section. The scalar motive reappears, however, to close the entire motet, and there Josquin alters his part writing, particularly in the bassus, to prepare the convergence more

Ex. 12-3. *Continued*

decisively (ex. 12-3). The medial cadence (downbeat, m. 65) is marked by significant convergence, but once more it is sudden, in the coordination not only of durations but of root identities. The E triad succeeds two different triads in three dimensions. The final cadence, by contrast, converges its hierarchical progressions as well as durations. In sacrificing the complete scale in the bassus at the very end, Josquin unites his three root levels in a single triad, all of which resolve to the conclusive A triad together. His plagal motions in the surface dimensions evaporate the remaining tensions of the motet.

Neither the beginning nor ending sections of the tertia pars of "Miserere mei, Deus," take any advantage of imitative paired voices or any other subdivision of the texture, the mainstay of Renaissance structural articulation. Indeed, the mystical effect Josquin seeks depends on a full texture, as does, of course, any convincing ending in his style. For the inner articulations, therefore, he depends on his masterful counterpoint, which can unmake cadences as they are made, can intensify a texture internally without disrupting the surface, and can conjure the illusion of three successions of harmonies going on at once. The opening is a textbook case of a master wringing the utmost from the potentials of a musical language.[2] Without harmonic function, there is yet harmonic shape in the rhythm. Locating the focal stream in the phenomenal rhythm is both cause and effect of his mystical sound, and it allows Josquin to make of the root motions a steady acceleration over nine measures that lets up only at the last, undergirding a brilliantly wrought texture that exploits every aspect of his harmonic language.

MOZART: OVERTURE TO *THE MARRIAGE OF FIGARO*

If Josquin's secret is to focus attention on minute changes in the surface, Mozart's secret, at the beginning of this overture, is to ban harmony from the surface altogether. If Josquin maximizes his harmonic resources, Mozart appears to waste them: *Figaro* opens without any phenomenal harmonic rhythm at all (ex 12-4).

For a long time I have wondered about the sudden fortissimo in measure 12. Why does it sound so rightly placed yet with a touch of playful surprise about it, perfect for the Italian opera buffa? It is not a cadential harmony. In fact, in the most abstract hearing, the harmony has not budged off the tonic since the first notes. There is no change in any root motion from measure 11 to 12. There is no other stupendous change to warrant such an explosion. Yet in its raw excitement it is completely convincing.

Of course, the triadic fanfares in measures 9 and 11 point to the high D_6 like an arrow. Was there ever a passage more congenial to Leonard Meyer's ideas about melodic implications? The graph in example 12-5 shows how structural pitch patterns on two levels in the woodwind melody converge (in Meyer's sense) on the high D_6. The downbeat placement, registral prominence, and sheer duration of the goal tone allow it to realize the implied continuations generated in the previous measures.[3] The length of the D_6 also conforms to the small group patterns established in measures 8–9 and then 10–11, which show up in the phenomenal graph (ex. 12-4). Undoubtedly these features of the woodwind melody justify the fortissimo to a great extent, but not entirely. It would be too easy a construction. Everyone could write a terrific fortissimo that way.

Looking to the dimensional graph to find something a little more ingenious, the eye fixes immediately on the column of whole notes on measure 12. Yes, it stands out from its neighbors, but this measure is not an instance of harmonic convergence, for its dimensions, despite appearances, do not really move together. The bass pitch is just starting a long duration;

Ex. 12-4. Mozart, Overture to *The Marriage of Figaro*, mm. 1–18.

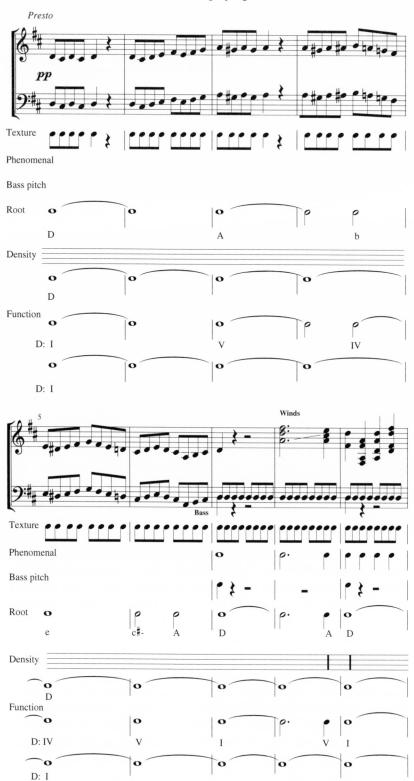

Ex. 12-4. *Continued*

the first-level root is just finishing one. The higher-level root and function simply sustain right through, as if nothing has happened. For them, nothing has.

The subtleties in the harmonic rhythm begin with *Figaro*'s famous unison opening: a harmonic texture that excludes phenomenal rhythm and bass pitch rhythm altogether. It is a single melody, highly constrained in its range. There is no special harmonic role for the bass; it goes with everyone else. And since we hear only one note at time, can we speak of harmony at all? Well, yes and no. In the strictly perceived, objective harmony that is the concern of phenomenal rhythm, there is nothing, no chords at all, no simultaneous combinations of pitches. But in the more imaginary, abstract realms of roots and their functions, Mozart's melodies do imply harmonic backgrounds that change audibly. So here is the strange situation where the abstracted harmonic changes are more real than the surface ones; indeed, surface harmonic rhythm does not really exist.

Of course such imagined roots and functions are imprecise articulations, fuzzy and quite unlike fully textured changes. Thus, particularly in the first-

Ex. 12-4. *Continued*

level root and function graphs, there is more latitude than usual about exactly where the changes occur. (I have placed them all on principal beats because of the tendency of listeners to organize important articulations around such metric markers.) But this very imprecision accounts for much of the credibility in Mozart's seven-bar phrase. It is a great example of one of his illusions of classical symmetry, a phrase that sounds balanced when it is not. The function graph shows how the syntax accelerates its members so that the final tonic arrives on a strong beat one measure ahead of schedule, but even this explanation is a simplification. Much depends on calculated ambiguity of both harmony and meter, so that the early arrival of D in measure 7 must be welcomed as both cadence and downbeat. Perhaps this asymmetry, in some very abstract sense of phrase rhythm, contributes a modicum to the bit of surprise in measure 12, which arrives at least one bar, perhaps two, ahead of its own balance point.

Ex. 12-5. Implication-realization graph of the woodwind melody from Mozart, Overture to *The Marriage of Figaro*, mm. 8–12.

The lack of phenomenal and bass pitch rhythm has two other effects. The first is to forbid hypermeter—the sensation that in this very fast piece, not just half-note beats but whole measures may alternately take on relations of strong and weak. Every measure in the first seven seems accented. Thereafter the polyphony begins to accent measures but so inconsistently as to exacerbate the ambiguity. The newly independent bass voice accents measures 7, 9, and 11 while the pattern of the woodwind fanfare (mm. 8–12) weights 8 and 10. The fortissimo, then, is metrically both strong and weak, a kind of expected surprise, a rather delightful sensation.

When they make their first appearance in measure 7, the bass pitch and phenomenal rhythms invite the listener's attention as a radical change of texture, the second effect. Even when the first-level root rhythm becomes explicit through the woodwind fanfare, a case can be made for a bifocal stream here with the phenomenal, owing to Mozart's orchestration. He insists, despite the simplicity of the progression, on four real wind parts. This gives the phenomenal rhythm a very high density, which emphasizes its speed, much faster than the root. But the listener's concentration is released with the grand chord (m. 12). No, the column of whole notes in measure 12 does not represent true convergence, but it is nonetheless a unique moment where all the harmonic rhythms are motionless, a kind of suspended breathing space for the texture before harmonic independence accelerates.

The fortissimo's logic derives from preceding melodic and phenomenal harmonic implications, its taint of surprise from metric ones and from the unexpectedly new openness of the texture. It is not an especially powerful moment, but it is a brilliant one, created from a virtually stable harmony by merely moving within it. But the brilliance is superficial, like many of the moments in the aria of the opera's stuffy lawyer (no. 4, "La vendetta") soon to be heard. The real brilliance, uniting both string and wind colors, follows on, and here the dimensional graph is true to form: stratification (mm. 13–16) followed by an increase in speed and strong convergence driving to the cadence.

Ex. 12-6. Debussy, Prelude no. 1 ("Danseuses de Delphes").

DEBUSSY: PRELUDE NO. 1
("DANSEUSES DE DELPHES")

Although one of Debussy's piano preludes has already been visited in the context of non-functional harmony (chapter 11), this first prelude (ex. 12-6) offers a different problem for harmonic rhythm. Here is a composition where conventionally spelled triads act according to conventional syntax in some passages while others adopt quite different syntaxes. How does one texture proceed to another, and what unites such radically different harmonic approaches? What can harmonic rhythm have to do with the interaction of different harmonic systems?

The prelude is, among other things, a grand experiment in the denaturing of traditional harmonic functions, a process of weakening and dissolving their proper grammatical roles right before our ears so that the most elemental sounds take on new meaning.[4] The process is not a steady advance, being rather more like two steps forward and one back, but it begins with the very first gesture, three chords that harmonize a rhythmic dance motive in the alto voice (m. 1). Already harmonic rhythm affects Debussy's altered functions. By measure 2 the meter is quite clear, which tells us that the F augmented triad must be understood as an altered dominant. The bass pitch and weak beat placement overpower the misspelling, although the augmented chord does significantly weaken the traditional dominant tension with ambiguity. On the other hand, no sooner is this skewed dominant taught to us than it is replaced at the end of the phrase by a traditional dominant (m. 5). Fortunately, the displaced tonic function in measure 4 and the eighth-note root rhythm confuse the meter sufficiently to rob that F major triad of upbeat/dominant associations, creating a pervading air of mystery about it.

This sense affects the next phrase (mm. 6–10), really a close variant of the first animated by offbeat chords, but that simple change drastically reduces the density of the root changes. The security of the opening functions is gone, and even though the second phrase ends as the first, the denaturing has begun.

The next phrase (mm. 11–14) brings the next step in the process. The F dominant persists through as a pedal, but the music above reduces the syntax of triads to Debussy's parallelisms, triad melodies if you will, moving in traditional contrary motion to the dance rhythms in the top. Because these give no priority to the F major triad, the function of the pedal weakens steadily until measure 13, where it is banished entirely by Debussy's choices of roots. The F_2 and F_3 maintain a link with the pedal's origin by pure sonority, but they have virtually no other effect, and the apparent stratification in the graph is mostly illusion.

Now that triadic syntax has dissolved away, Debussy designs another for the fourth phrase (mm. 15–20). It is quite a simple syntax: harmonize unison pitch-class sounding on the beat with a major triad with its root a perfect fifth below on the offbeat. Then this breaks down, replaced by abstract roots on F and C and finally F once more. The fifth phrase (mm. 21–24) brings yet another design: onbeat unisons are harmonized with major triads with roots a major third below for offbeats, and this syntax is perfectly consistent for four measures.[5] The final phrase recapitulation propounds augmented chords, the one on F resuming its newly defined weak dominant function. Debussy clearly uses decelerating harmonic speed to effect the principal resolution; the last chords attain stability through sheer duration more than anything else.

In summary, the first and last phrases act as twin pillars between which traditional syntax is denatured into a number of experimental syntaxes that

Ex. 12-6. *Continued*

are bound together with the dance motive and the offbeat texture introduced in the second phrase. How does harmonic rhythm participate in this
denaturing process?

One feature stands out in a bird's-eye view of the entire graph: each
new phrase reduces the number of active dimensions. Debussy opens with
six, typical of fully functional harmony. The first new phrase at measure 11
cuts out the lower-level function, since those triads give up their normal
relations for parallel motion. Then function dies away altogether, and the
next phrase (mm. 15–20) exploits intermittently first-level and then quite
abstract second-level root motions. The end of that phrase produces a
strange effect of harmonic integration that the dimensional graph cannot
quite capture, as both root motions intertwine. In other words, although
the faster motion is placed above as usual, it is difficult to hear which is
an abstraction of the other—or perhaps both are? In melodic terms, this
would be heterophony, and the upshot is that there is far less divergence
than appears, and perhaps one fewer dimension. Finally, the climactic fifth

Ex. 12-6. *Continued*

phrase (mm. 21–24) shows the leanest harmonic rhythm of all, and it is a strange, haunting kind of climax indeed, if that is the right word. Here Debussy's artificial syntax could not be more consistent, yet as the tones rise ever higher, the effect of the harmonic rhythm is to dissolve away to nothing, owing to that very consistency. Measure 21 begins with syncopated root rhythm as the offbeats change and clarify the best guesses that the unisons force on us. By the end of bar 22, certainly by 23, we have learned the scheme. And the effect of that learning? Root identities fall now on the downbeat, reducing the speed and tension of syncopation. Density plummets to minimum, and then all trace of the bass is lost. Exactly when this happens is impossible to say, and that is really the point of this experiment. As the texture reduces to two bare harmonic motions, the upward progression of thirds promises to go on forever, beyond the limits of audibility. This is no resolution in any traditional sense, merely dissolution, perhaps annihilation.

Ex. 12-6. Continued

Ex. 12-6. *Continued*

The recapitulation of the opening subsists on nothing but unisons and augmented triads until the very last chord, but after the previous adventures they seem like old friends, even the weird dominant. With functions so weak, Debussy ends the piece with means that would have been quite familiar to his medieval and Renaissance forebears who composed with non-functional languages: gradual slowing of speed, increasing convergence, even a reminiscence of a plagal effect in the bass.

One could say with some justice that in this case the harmonic rhythm of Prelude no. 1 does not "participate" in the denaturing of functional harmony but only reflects the process and provides a means of describing its effects. Taken to extremes, this argument could apply to any traditional analysis, too; after all, harmonic rhythm arises only from combinations of tones. But here it does seem that Debussy's experiments in syntax are driving the effects of harmonic rhythm rather than vice versa. Debussy does not exploit speed or independence in his most adventurous phrases to accomplish musical goals, only at the beginning and the end, but those qualities are nonetheless produced by what he does with his inventions and thus hold a mirror to some of their musical effects. In this indirect manner harmonic rhythm can explain some of the peculiarly evocative sensations arising from the obscure realm of Debussy's personal language.

Ex. 12-6. *Continued*

BACH: PRELUDIO FROM THE
PARTITA IN E MAJOR FOR
SOLO VIOLIN

The compositions of J. S. Bach for solo flute, cello, and violin are the most famous instrumental monophonies in the history of Western music. They are such a treasure for the players of those instruments that they could not help but provoke the jealousy of other musicians, who plundered them ruthlessly and now play them within conservatory walls on every instrument from archlute to xylophone. Their fame among historians and critics, and their ability to hold a proud place on so many recital programs in an essentially polyphonic culture, stems from their uncanny projection of traditional harmonic syntax, complete with bass and voice-leading, that ac-

Ex. 12-6. *Continued*

companies the rich dance tunes or brilliant bariolages. Analysts have always pointed to the compound melody to account for this sensation, Bach's exploitation of rhythm, register, and the perceptual proclivities of listeners to conjure the illusion of polyphony. But if these monophonies do indeed project a virtual polyphony, they must also project harmonic rhythm. That it does not exist on the surface of the music poses no obstacle. As Mozart's overture and most of the other passages cited have shown, a stream of harmonic rhythm produced in part with the willing aid of the listener's imagination is just as real as one deduced purely from acoustic phenomena. Such imagination affects the analyst's task profoundly, to say nothing of the composer's. Indeed, the control of harmonic rhythm through a single melody could represent a summit of Bach's contrapuntal power.

Even when it projects compound melody, monophony eliminates or redefines the surface dimensions of harmonic rhythm. When there is one

Ex. 12-7. J. S. Bach, Preludio from Partita in E Major for Solo Violin, mm. 1–29.

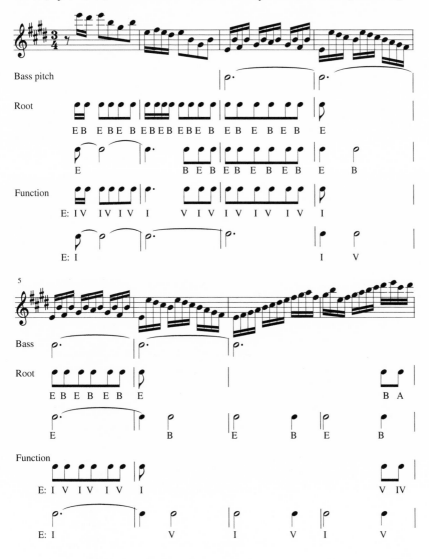

note at a time, the score will reflect faithfully the textural rhythm through-out, obviating that graph. Phenomenal rhythm is absent, since there are no acoustic chords. The bass pitch dimension, explicitly represented by a distinct instrumental color and register at most times, now comes and goes, more from Bach's treatment of pitches on the lower strings of the violin than from any specific range.

The more abstract dimensions of root and function appear in all their accustomed glory; indeed, Bach's allusive counterpoint makes imagining

Ex. 12-7. *Continued*

distinct harmonic levels quite easy for experienced listeners, one of the joys of this music. Three levels of root rhythm are not infrequent. (See ex. 12-7, Partita for Solo Violin.)

The opening few bars show what an unrestrained imagination can hear. How can that innocent figure in the first measure be anything more than a tonic arpeggio? Harmonized, it probably would be, but alone, its features take on extraordinary significance. The brief leading-tone D-sharp$_5$, the most powerful melodic symbol of dominant function, prepares the same perception of the two B$_4$s, both metrically weak, as functioning dominants should be. If the graph in the first-level root and function dimensions seems

Ex. 12-7. *Continued*

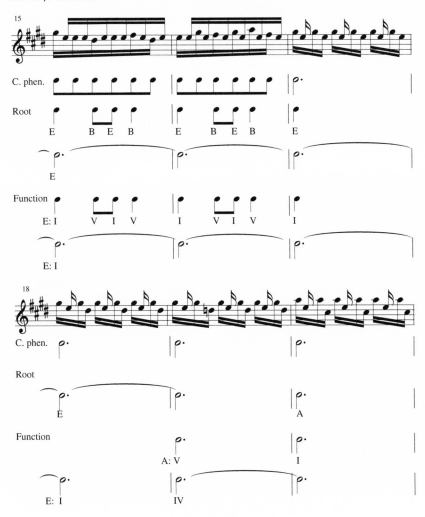

too detailed to be credible, try realizing it at the keyboard; it works reasonably well. And none of this contradicts the simultaneous impression that, yes, the innocent figure is indeed a tonic arpeggio.[6]

Hierarchical levels, never precise to begin with, are vaguer still in this music. By the fourth measure, when the first scales diminish the harmonic significance of sixteenth-note motion, a slower, more abstract root rhythm arises. Clearly the second measure has some relevance here, with its turn figure that provides the first step-motion, but the lines between first- and second-level root rhythm are blurry indeed. This reflects the dynamic of compound melody itself. The number of voices is never consistent and the boundaries between one-, two-, and three-voice textures are seldom explicit.

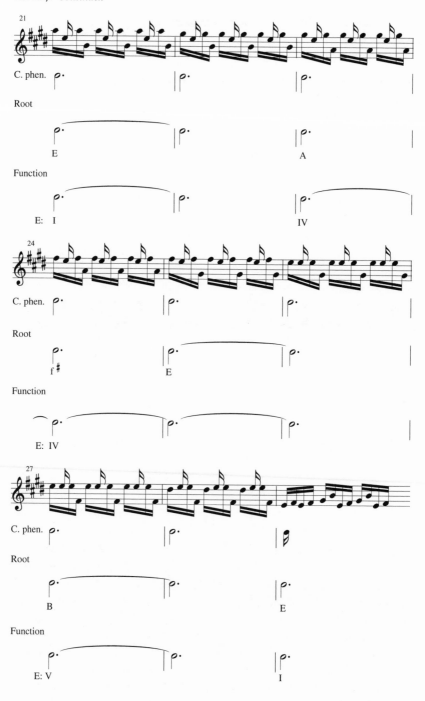

The blending of one motion into another is part of the fascination of Bach's solo instrument writing.

In measure 3 Bach's first pedal tone appears on B_4, and that E_4 is a "bass" seems confirmed in the following bars, when the scales spring from it as a point of reference. This is indeed the lowest E on the violin, and once Bach forsakes it for the higher register after measure 7, the bass pitch dimension disappears.

In a composition so dependent on the perception of compound melody we should expect a prominent dimension of contrapuntal phenomenal harmonic rhythm (see chapter 3), even if the proper phenomenal rhythm has no place. Curiously, Bach reserves this element. The opening bars show isolated instances of explicit compound melody (mm. 3, 5, 9, 11, 12), but their rhythm is never independent of the root rhythm until bar 13, so there seems to be little point in cluttering the graph. With Bach's spectacular exploitation of the open E string, however, the contrapuntal phenomenal rhythm achieves independence and smooths a most remarkable transition: suddenly in measure 17, the texture opens up and relaxes the pace in every dimension except the ceaseless sixteenths actually played by the violin. The contrapuntal phenomenal rhythm becomes the sole articulator of the measure while Bach completely changes the dynamic of the music. The furious kinetic activity converts to slowly mounting tensions of harmonic function and independence. The functions articulate the first important cadence in measure 29, but while this complete syntax plays out, the degree of independence actually falls. The arrival on bar 29, in the "bass" register, completes an opening statement, not a climax.

This statement is a masterful lesson in the prolongation of fundamental harmonies through two distinct textures. Bach establishes the active, detailed motions first, so that we believe in their integrity; otherwise they might be mere elaborations of structural harmonic progressions. These more abstract rhythms he saves to introduce afterward and establishes their own integrity with a complete syntax. Now the terms of understanding his monophony are set.

The cadence in measure 29 begins an excursus organized around the key of the relative minor, C-sharp. After a brief transition (mm. 53–60), this enormous tonal dipole (E major/C-sharp minor) is transposed, almost in its entirety, to A major/F-sharp minor.

Example 12-8 picks up from the last cadence in that section.

One controversial feature of this dimensional graph would be the fastest stream of root motion from measure 119 onward. But while the audibility of the sixteenth notes as roots is certainly contestable, more speaks for it than against. Bach has worked hard, from the very first motive, to have us imagine tiny gestures harmonically. The credibility of these quick changes is revived in the measures (mm. 109–119) when intermittent pedals

Ex. 12-8. J. S. Bach, Preludio from Partita in E Major for Solo Violin, mm. 109–130.

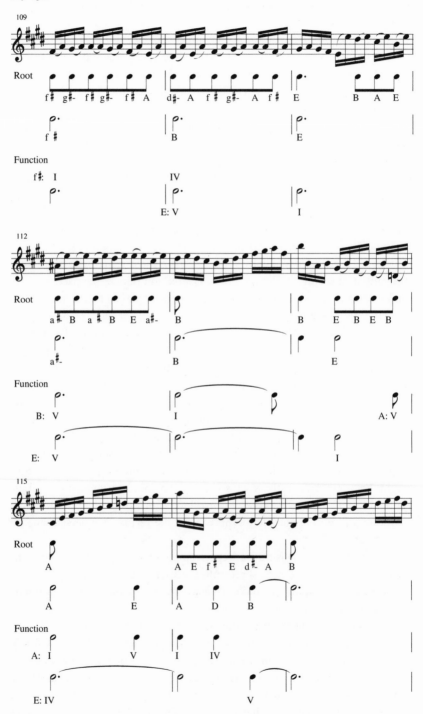

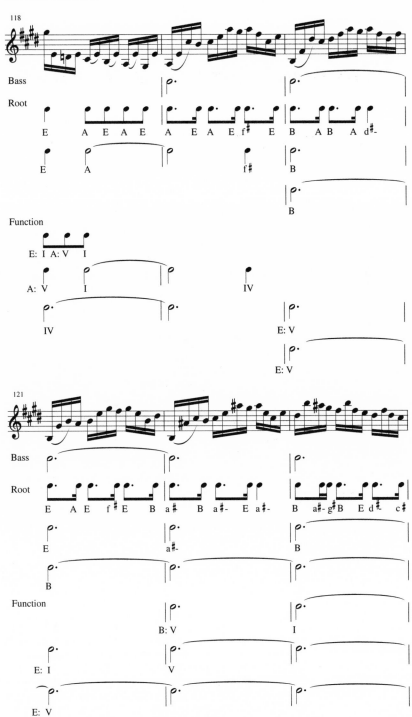

181

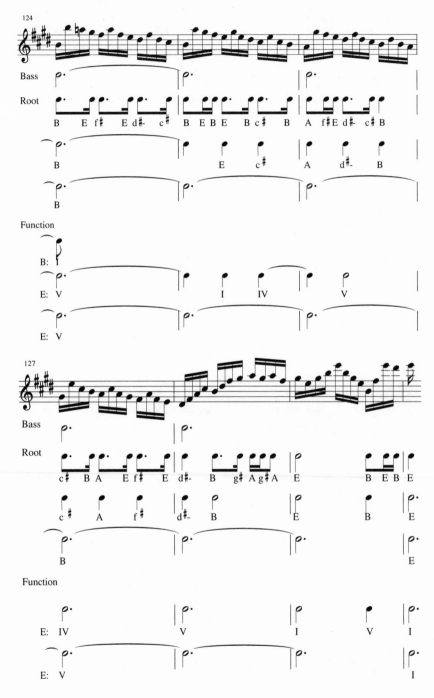

create easily perceptible roots as they have throughout. Now, late in the piece, he designs a new figure whose span across three strings of the violin on every downbeat (mm. 119–122) dissociates the fourth sixteenth in a manner most unneighborly. The composer need not always have the last word about how to hear his own music, but neither is his view to be dismissed out of hand; in his autograph Bach slurs the three sixteenths together just here and nowhere else. But here, as ever in this work, the graph portrays what may be imagined.

Whether one hears the fastest root motions or not, the rest of the dimensional graph speaks for itself about the power of the climax in this prelude. As the tonality returns home, there is no simple recap of a ritornello theme. Instead the embedded functions pile up, creating a bewildering but generally increased web of harmonic independence. To make the final drive, Bach transforms his descending motive into a cascade of diverse harmonic implications that radically increases the speed of the focal stream (m. 125), adding to the strain against the long, long dominant pedal. Convergence occurs like a planetary alignment with the first explicit tonic arpeggiation, to reiterate one measure later with the metric emphasis on the high E_6. Rare must be the violinist who can resist stretching the beats in those marvelous measures.

Convergence in a monophony cannot be total since the action of the voices is realized over time. This must be why, in the little codetta that follows example 12-8, Bach halts the motoric sixteenths to have the violinist play real polyphony, that is, triple and quadruple stop chords, to make a stronger convergence on the final cadence (mm. 134–136). Then there is nothing but a final flourish of speed rushing up to the high E where it all began.

EPILOGUE

*H*AVING SAMPLED what the dimensional technique of harmonic rhythm can tell us about individual passages, we can now step back and review some general lessons of analyzing harmonic rhythm. What should one keep in mind when reading a dimensional graph, or even when deciding whether to take the trouble to make one?

The analyses in the previous chapter and the other major analyses show unequivocally that assessments of a passage's harmonic rhythm profit most when made in conjunction with other critical evaluations. Harmonic rhythm rarely determines the shape of a work by itself; rather, it is part of the fabric of musical syntax in polyphonic musical languages. Its tensions and textures contribute to the whole effect without slighting any of the other manifold musical wonders that are rightly prized. In the same way, analytical methods that focus on melody or form or even other aspects of harmony and rhythm do not generally contest or exclude dimensional analysis. Dimensional analysis does not supplant other traditional approaches; it complements them, and that is one of its strengths.

The most interesting interpretations come from the dimensional analysis taken as a whole rather than from any single one of its dimensions. Since harmony is a multidimensional aspect of musical experience, it is only reasonable that our fascination with it might come from the interrelations of those various dimensions that, like the several colors of a painter's palette, can combine into a virtual infinity of effects. Therefore disagreements over individual single analytical decisions will hardly ever affect the broad interpretation very much, particularly in the matter of naming the changes. Other analysts might reasonably criticize my naming a certain chord as F-sharp minor rather than A major or assigning a IV instead of a I. But there is apt to be much less disagreement over the fact that the triad or function has changed at those points than over what to call them, and it is the fact of the change that counts in harmonic rhythm. Of course details are important, particularly as they add up, and care must be exercised always, but the broad interpretation of harmonic rhythm will not turn on a few controversial local decisions.

The perceptive analyst will be ready to adapt the dimensional technique to the situation at hand. The basic assumptions of dimensional technique are sufficiently general that their application in graphing can fit the particular musical language in question, even a peculiar utterance within a language. When triads are absent, as in Machaut, when function disappears, as in Debussy, when the harmony is merely abstract, as in Bach's monophony, the graph must reflect the harmonic premises of those conditions. No one pretends by saying this that all musical languages are harmonically equivalent or that the harmonic aspect of all languages is equally worthy, or some other vacuous relativism. The graph shows the harmonic potential, that is, what could change in the harmonic aspect of any situation, no more and no less. How to weigh that information in a more panoramic view of the music is then the province of good criticism.

Respecting the premises of a specific musical language or situation is as much an opportunity as a limitation. The evaluation of the harmonic element in early music in particular has been retarded, despite the upswell in the performance of this rich and beautiful repertory, because of a circumspect reluctance to apply the concepts of Rameau and Riemann anachronistically and because of an overzealous reverence for the terminologies of medieval and Renaissance theorists (e.g., if they never wrote the word "triad" then neither can we). I would hope that the analyses of Machaut, Dufay, and Josquin presented here might demonstrate that the essential aspects of their diverse musical languages can operate as the premises of a harmonic analysis, so that the resulting criticism enlightens the perceptions of music lovers who love their music today. Harmonic rhythm must be an essential feature of their musical textures, if only because it seems impossible to believe that these great contrapuntists combined their melodies without a thought about the timing of changes in those vertical sonorities for which they had no names but which nevertheless shaped their listeners' musical experience.

Even the immediate context of a single composition can color the interpretation. Remember how important a role the phenomenal harmonic rhythm played in generating the tensions of Vivaldi's "Winter" Concerto (ex. 10-3) while the same dimension in Chopin served chiefly as a textural color (ex. 9-4). The complete dimensional graph gives every harmonic aspect its due, and this can make every harmonic aspect seem perceptually equivalent. They are not. The relative saliences of the dimensions differ from piece to piece, passage to passage, even moment to moment. Skillful interpretation takes all this into account.

The passages and movements analyzed in this book are mostly short ones because the dimensional method is most likely to have the most interesting things to say about the immediate details of music. Structures spanning durations greater than a minute or so will principally exploit dynamics other than harmonic rhythm. The reasons for this are perceptual and cognitive. The dynamics of harmonic rhythm—speed and independence for the most part—depend on the listener's awareness of precise comparative durations. Obviously, the listener must be able to sense whether harmonic events are becoming shorter or longer in order to feel the concomitant musical tensions. Human working memory limits that ability to relatively short spans; we can sense acceleration when a harmony lasting four seconds is followed by one lasting three, but when a pedal lasting twenty seconds is followed by one lasting fifteen, most people will simply hear both pedals as "long." The tensions of harmonic rhythm are transient, lived from moment to moment, utterly different in quality from, say, the lack of full texture, or the state of music in a foreign key, both of which have more synchronic, long-range effects.

Of course, when a dimensional graph is synchronically interpreted for its definition of harmonic texture rather than for its charting of the ebbs and flows of tension, it can certainly characterize long spans of time, as it did with Bach's E Major Partita for Solo Violin. For here we identify the music with a certain quality or state of being, which, like that of a foreign key, can persist for minutes on end before it is contrasted. In that case dimensional analysis is more concerned with "what kind of music" than with "what happens in the music."

Clearly, "what happens in the music" has occupied most of my attention here. Some might wonder at the virtual equation of the dynamic qualities emerging from harmonic rhythm with musical tension and resolution. My aesthetic stance on this point is quite straightforward. As I have argued in *Musical Languages* and elsewhere, there can be no musical language without syntax, and syntax has two essential roles in any language: first, to organize information, that is, to provide the means for structure, and second, to mediate the tensions and resolutions of the music through its compositional techniques.[1] Tension is a musical essence, and the composer's control of musical tensions in their multiplicity, their

arising and subsiding, their blending and converting from one kind to another, their semantic interactions, their resolution or even annihilation,
stands at the center of musical art. If one indispensable aspect of that art
in the western tradition is harmonic rhythm, it is because harmonic
rhythm is so much a part of those things.

NOTES

1. For more details about how to use dimensional theory as a pedagogical tool, see my article "Teaching Harmonic Rhythm."

1. *Harmonic Practice*, 77.

2. Of course, this independence is relative, not absolute. The harmonic rhythm of a St. Martial organum, for example, cannot move faster than the fastest-moving voice, a constraint that applies to all harmonic rhythms since.

3. See Lester, *Compositional Theory in the Eighteenth Century*, 113. See also Caplin's survey of many of Rameau's followers: "Theories of Harmonic-Metric Relationships from Rameau to Riemann." Rameau's advice is reiterated by the twentieth-century composer Roger Sessions in his *Harmonic Practice*, 89.

4. Arlin attributes the first explicit definition to Piston (see note 5). See "Harmonic Rhythm in Selected Fugues," 6.

5. *Harvard Dictionary of Music*, 319.

6. Chap. 5.

7. Some of the more outstanding examples: LaRue, "Harmonic Rhythm in the Beethoven Symphonies"; Arlin, "Harmonic Rhythm in Selected Fugues"; Davis, "Harmonic Rhythm in Mozart's Sonata Form."

8. I assume the simplest kind of durational analysis, analogous to Piston's, and also that the melody is played or sung with relatively constant timbre. A new instrument entering midway introduces another type of change, another dimension that complicates the analysis.

9. In *Musical Languages*, chap. 4, I argue that musical languages are rarely

context-free languages and that judgments about individual events must take into account their unique contextual environments.

10. If definition is necessary, I would fall back on the "cluster concept," a favorite technique in philosophy, whereby essential characteristics of the thing to be defined are listed, requiring not that all of them be present in any instance but rather only a cluster of them.

CHAPTER 2

1. See Lester, *The Rhythms of Tonal Music*, 6, for more on composite rhythm. It is with some reluctance that I introduce the neologism "textural rhythm" to stand in for "composite rhythm" and only for these two reasons: "composite rhythm" is not at all widely used in criticism or analysis, from which I conclude that the term is not widely known; and "textural rhythm" speaks directly to the source of the perception, the texture of the music, whereas a "composite rhythm" could arise from any number of musical compounds, such as the composite rhythm of the tutti and soli in a concerto, for example.

2. The one possible exception to this theorem would be the case of a harmonic event, such as a dominant pedal, that is sustained so long that it acquires the stability of a tonic and thus changes its harmonic function. Imagine a G major triad in a C major context. It has dominant function, of course, and the listener experiences a harmonic tension, awaiting its resolution to the tonic. But if this G major triad is sustained so long that the perceiving mind loses track of the key of C major, forgets the triad's dominant function, and begins to regard it as a stable tonic in G major, then its function has changed from dominant to tonic, a change that should be recognized in the dimensional graph of harmonic rhythm and, according to the theorem, in the textural rhythm. But no new note, no new attack, has sounded, so it cannot be indicated.

This kind of rhythmic change is quite unlike the precisely timed kind that we normally hear as "rhythm." Some writers would not even admit it as a rhythm because this change is not discrete but rather like that of a crescendo. Just as there will be no unanimous agreement as to when the soft becomes loud, there will be none as to when the dominant pedal changes its function to a tonic. Furthermore, this complication of textural rhythm is extremely rare and so need not derail this project. A notation to take care of it will be suggested in chapter 7.

3. More precisely, the textural rhythm of the opening measure is *represented* by traditional notation of sixteenth notes. I hope readers will forgive the imprecision of this common abbreviation, which I will use freely from here on.

4. When graphing the textural rhythm of a case like this, it really doesn't matter whether a note-head or a rest is used, since it is the duration of changes that interests us. However, a rest may symbolize the reason behind the graph.

5. Certainly the phenomenologists would hold this view. See Clifton, *Music as Heard*.

CHAPTER 3

1. Lester, *Compositional Theory in the Eighteenth Century*, chap. 4.
2. This literature is enormous. For a review, see Butler, *The Musician's Guide to*

Perception and Cognition, chap. 7, and Dowling and Harwood, *Music Cognition,* chaps. 5–6.

3. One of the earliest such studies is Diana Deutsch, "Octave generalization and tune recognition."

4. Schumann, "12 Etüden für Pianoforte von Friedrich Chopin. Werk 25," 73.

5. More recently its foundations have been analyzed in the psychologist's laboratory. There it is often called "melodic streaming," and its effectiveness depends on the speed of the melody, the size of the intervals between the voices, and the consistency of presentation. See Butler, *The Musician's Guide to Perception and Cognition,* chap. 7.

6. One could argue quite reasonably that the onset of each voice is in fact a change, but that approach only replicates the phenomenal graph. I have taken the slightly more liberal view of hearing the virtual four-voice texture retrospectively (see chapter 5, note 6).

CHAPTER 4

1. For a survey of these writers and their methods, see Lester, *Compositional Theory in the Eighteenth Century,* chap. 3.

2. This principle comes from the Gestalt school of psychology, was first applied to visual perception, and is variously known as the Law of Good Continuation, Good Form, and Prägnanz. Leonard Meyer applied Gestalt perception to his first theory of *Emotion and Meaning in Music,* and it has been widely cited in many forms in other theories of music. There is also an enormous scientific literature that supports this kind of perception. For an introduction see Butler, *The Musician's Guide to Perception and Cognition,* chap. 7, and Dowling and Harwood, *Music Cognition,* chap. 6.

3. From his first edition of *Harmony.*

4. Page 79.

5. Arguments about the essential and uneliminable role of context may be found in my book *Musical Languages,* chap. 4.

6. See the discussion of this tradition in Crist, "Aria Forms," 71.

CHAPTER 5

1. Piston used a system of all upper-case Roman numerals, which does not indicate triad quality, a rather serious deficiency in view of the many times when the sole harmonic change is, say, from the major version of a triad to its minor. But many Roman numeral systems in use today, of course, adopt a case system with additions similar to those used here.

2. I call this view "modern" because multivalent theories seem to stem from the work of Leonard B. Meyer (see especially *Explaining Music*) and Eugene Narmour (see *Beyond Schenkerism* for a concise articulation of this position). Of course the notion of a multilayered analysis came to prominence in the twentieth century through the work of Heinrich Schenker, but in fact such analyses date back at least to the eighteenth century. For example see Mattheson, *Der vollkommene Kapellmeister,* 673–674.

3. A fuller discussion of feedback perception as it relates to music is in my *Musical Languages,* chap. 4.

4. Actually the sources do not indicate which instrument is to play the top line, but most authorities believe the transverse flute to be the likeliest choice. For simplicity I simply refer to that melody as the "flute melody."

5. In general, rests are never written in the graph of the root/quality dimension unless a silence in the entire texture (general rest) is so long that the listener cannot make the connection from the last-sounded chord to the first one after the rest.

6. Current estimates of the mind's "working memory," a model for its capacity to hold percepts in raw, uninterpreted, and complete states, run from 2 to 4 seconds. This is more than enough time to "listen back" half a beat. In fact it is this temporary store that explains the feedback perception mechanisms. Different levels or streams of information can affect one another's interpretation because, for that short time, they can interact while still taking in new information. For a review, see Berz, "Working Memory in Music."

7. Arguments for this version would rely on the listener's capacity to listen retrospectively for a few seconds, as described in note 6.

CHAPTER 6

1. If one enlarges the harmonic vocabulary beyond triads, which may well be appropriate for Debussy's musical language, and includes chords with an "added sixth," then the soprano note G_4 would articulate the chord and raise the density one count.

2. This flexibility in density criteria allows different graphs to reflect different points of view about the analysis. If one established a criteria of regularly including added sixth and seventh factors into Debussy's harmonic vocabulary, in the sense of contributing to chord identity for the listener, then a different density graph would result. But the notion of density as an image of the amount of emphasis that each chord change receives remains intact.

3. Other writers have invoked the notion of density in theoretical writing about rhythm. Maury Yeston discusses the "density of simultaneous attacks or the density of simultaneous patterns" in *Stratification of Musical Rhythm*, 46. Joel Lester comes close to the definition used here when he writes: "One type of textural accent is caused by attacks in many or all voices of a texture. These points of density are accented in relation to those points at which only one of a few voices have attacks"; *The Rhythms of Tonal Music*, 29.

4. This occurrence is highly unlikely in Corelli's musical language. However, it can make the theoretical point, which has significant relevance elsewhere: that dissonance can make a change of triad less perceptible, which by definition decreases the density of the triad change.

5. Two pitch-classes are necessary to create a local context for the identification of a root. These pitch-classes will make the interval of a third, fourth, fifth, or sixth (e.g., C–E or C–E♭ is C triad; C–F is F triad; C–G is C triad; C–A♭ is A♭ triad; C–A is A triad). If another pitch-class is added that makes one of these consonant intervals with either of the two already present, we will have immediately an alternative root interpretation. Only if a pitch-class can make a dissonant second or seventh interval with both pitch-classes already present might the addition not disturb the triad identity.

Here are the relevant cases (0–11 pitch-class notation):

1. Case of minor third (0–3) made by the first two notes; a third note is added between them at 1 or 2
2. Case of major third (0–4); a third note is added at 2
3. Case of minor sixth (0–8); a third note is added at 10
4. Case of major sixth (0–9); a third note is added at 11

But if the minor seventh (10) is allowed as a legitimate chord factor, all four cases are nullified, since its inversion is a major second (2). Interval 2 or 10 is found in each of the four cases, made between the third tone and one of the original two.

Therefore, any added pitch can conceivably suggest another chord, thus lowering the identifiability of a dissonant construction.

CHAPTER 7

1. Some writers call this system "tonality," a term I avoid using in this way because it seems to imply that other harmonic systems are "untonal" or "atonal" or otherwise operate without reference to a tonic, or tonal center. In most cases, of course, this is untrue.

2. "Plus l'art est contrôlé, limité, travaillé et plus il est libre." (The more art is controlled, limited, and worked over, the more it is free.) Stravinsky, *Poetics of Music*, 84.

3. For discussion of the syntactic tradeoffs made when musical languages evolve, see my *Musical Languages*, chaps. 2 and 7.

4. A "musical community" is a group of listeners for whom a certain perception is real and has practical value. In this case the relevant community might be called the community of "functional harmony perceivers." For more on this notion see my article "Musical Communities and Music Perception" and *Musical Languages*, chap. 7.

5. In particular, see *Musikalische Syntaxis* and *Vereinfachte Harmonielehre*. Theorists have recognized for a long time that triads signified by different Roman numerals can substitute for one another without changing the function: II for IV, VII for V, VI for I, and so forth. That is why Piston's symbology of seven numerals, while hinting at function, cannot explicitly indicate it.

6. Some writers call the subdominant function "dominant preparation."

7. Pages 192, 198.

8. The numerals are always in upper case; the quality of triad certainly affects function, but it is already shown in the root/quality graph. I decided not to introduce T, S, and D or other new symbols for these functions. It is true that many readers will have to remind themselves that the Roman numerals here do not mean what they mean in a traditional harmonic analysis, but the cognitive expense of that adjustment seemed small compared with learning a new set of symbols altogether. Besides, the association of I, IV, and V with generic tonic, subdominant, and dominant functions is hardly new and requires no radical retraining of old reading habits.

9. As with Bach's "Domine Deus" ritornello (see chap. 5), there will be some disagreement over the interpretation of the first measure. Some would not begin the higher function level that represents the pedal until bar 2 or even 3, when we are surer that it is, in fact, a pedal. Others might place it in the first measure, as

it is here, but delay the onset of the embedded level until the V arrives. I doubt that these small differences will affect the overall interpretation very much.

CHAPTER 8

1. *The Rhythms of Tonal Music*, 66; Fred Lerdahl and Ray Jackendoff also indicate that harmonic rhythm is the strongest factor in their model of metrical structure, *A Generative Theory*, 84–85.

2. In his book *Structural Functions of Music*, Wallace Berry postulates on page 330 that what he calls tonal function "is in and of itself *metrically neutral*," but he offers a very implausible example.

3. See note 2 to chapter 4.

4. There is high consensus on this point. Lester writes "Two separate components are thus necessary for the existence of a meter: a stream of beats or pulses, and an organization of those beats or pulses into accented and unaccented ones"; *The Rhythms of Tonal Music*, 45. Other theorists prefer to place the two elements in a hierarchical system. Maury Yeston writes that "meter is an outgrowth of the interaction of two levels—two differently-rated strata, the faster of which provides the elements and the slower of which groups them"; *Stratification of Musical Rhythm*, 66. See also Lerdahl and Jackendoff's model in *A Generative Theory*, chaps. 2, 4. For a recent and rather novel view of meter, however, see Hasty, *Meter as Rhythm*.

5. This is why barlines are maintained through the dimensional graph, although it must be always remembered that barlines do not create meter, as Beethoven has shown. They merely indicate the composer's belief about the prevailing meter.

6. The other function is the control of musical information. See my *Musical Languages*, chap. 2.

CHAPTER 9

1. That a performance of an unfamiliar composition, particularly one ending softly, may require the musicians to drop their arms before applause will begin is no counterexample to the traditional principle. The extramusical signal—dropping the arms—indicates the same fact as a chord that is known to be final: the last notes are over, and no more motion is to come.

2. A recent and comprehensive study of attention is Pashler, *The Psychology of Attention*. Particularly relevant to the capacity question are chaps. 3, 5, and 6.

3. Ibid., 157–162.

4. The issue of voluntary diversion and control of attention is complicated in the literature by differences over what constitutes truly sustained attention. See ibid., 242–251.

5. For a summary, see ibid., chap. 5.

6. Phonemes are not equivalent to the written letters. Thus, "e-d," as a past tense inflection, counts as one phoneme in these verbs because the two letters combine into one pronounced sound.

7. This phenomenon is known in psycholinguistics as "phonemic restoration." See Carroll, *The Psychology of Language*, 113.

8. Warren et al., "Melodic and Nonmelodic Sequences of Tones."

9. By citing such cognitive studies and data, I do not claim that all listeners will attend in exactly the same way, of course. Capacities of attention vary significantly among individuals and are affected by training and experience in the particular task being measured. The interpretations of harmonic rhythm in this book presuppose listeners who are reasonably experienced with the musical languages under discussion. But the perceptions of relatively inexperienced listeners, or, on the other hand, true experts such as Mozart, neither are irrelevant to this theory of harmonic rhythm nor limit it, for the dimensional graphs may be simplified or amplified to reflect the perceptual capacities of the musical community addressed. The principles remain the same. For more on this see my article "Musical Communities and Music Perception."

10. I regret using the word "phenomenal" once again in a different context, but after considering at length "superficial," "veridical," "surface," "fast," and "immediate," I believe that "phenomenal focal stream" best captures the essence of a perception that is more bottom-up than top-down, that is, requiring a minimum of abstraction. This connotation is the same one intended for the dimension of phenomenal harmonic rhythm: no abstract concept of triad need be applied. Applying a single connotation to different contexts is commonplace in music, as the terms "tonic," "exposition," "sonata," and many others readily show.

Of course, abstraction cannot be eliminated entirely, for even a single note is an abstraction to some extent, as is shown by the fact that no two C_3s are acoustically identical yet we think of them as "the same note." That is why the two contrastive terms introduced here—*phenomenal focal stream* and *abstract focal stream*—are relative terms, not exclusive antonyms.

11. "All things being equal" is the classic manner of taking care of the particulars that are bound to create contradictory cases. One might wonder, for example, why the extremely fast textural activity in Corelli's *Allegro* or Chopin's Etude would not distract the listening mind from the comparatively plodding triadic motions. They probably do, for a second or so, but the arpeggiated patterns in each case are so repetitive, so easily learned and predictable, that one can quickly turn to other matters. They color with brilliant rhythm the more variable and intrinsically interesting harmonic motions.

CHAPTER 10

1. Exceptions such as Bach's Cantata *Bw* 106 do exist. One significant group of exceptions would be those organ chorale preludes in which the cantus firmus drops out before a short postlude. The first of Bach's "Schübler" chorales, on "Wachet Auf," is a fine example, but these are still a minority of chorale preludes.

2. In this example the density of the phenomenal harmonic rhythm is graphed as well as the density of the root rhythm. This is often useful with early music. The reasons are explained in chapter 11.

3. For evidence on cognitive limits, applied to musical situations, see Lerdahl, "Cognitive Constraints on Compositional Systems"; William L. Berz, "Working Memory in Music;" and my article "The Need for Limits in Hierarchical Theories of Music."

4. For an argument for musical tensions that differ in kind, rather than simply in amount, see my *Musical Languages*, chap. 2.

CHAPTER 11

1. In the score for this graph and the one for example 11–2 I have omitted the text, "Kyrie eleison," in the interests of clarity. The change of syllables in the music may constitute important rhythm events but not harmonic ones; in addition, the text underlay in early music is imprecise in the extreme, so that to include the text would imply a certitude where none exists.

2. For more detail on such syntactic compensations in music, see my *Musical Languages*, chap. 2.

3. Inversions of the open fifth to an open perfect fourth may occur when a third voice sounds below them, making a triad of the sixth (e.g., m. 5). In such cases the root dimension denotes the name of the "root" pitch, as if the chord were not so inverted.

4. Another way to express this difference is to say that in dance music the distinction of strong and weak is felt clearly at the tactus beat, whereas in sacred music it is felt best at the subtactus levels.

5. It may be well to remember here that Machaut's manuscript has no measure lines at all; it records the voice parts separately, one note after another without division. This shows once again that the perception of meter does not arise from notation but from the phenomenal events of the sound itself.

6. For more on the isorhythmic technique in Machaut's mass, see Leech-Wilkinson, *Machaut's Mass*, 18–23.

7. If it is difficult to hear the cantus voice (top) cut off the half-note A_4 cleanly, then the textural/phenomenal rhythm becomes a whole note, more clearly convergent with the root rhythm.

8. Some way of weighting the various dimensions in the graph would certainly improve the method, but weighting perceptions is a notoriously difficult science, whose attempts with musical phenomena much simpler than harmonic rhythm have always come to grief.

CHAPTER 12

1. Two studies that explore the historical context contributing to this semantic are Macey, "Josquin's 'Miserere Mei, Deus,'" and Brothers, "Josquin's *Miserere.*"

2. In my view, this is the true source of musical style. See *Musical Languages*, chap. 8.

3. Here I apply Meyer's theory as it appears in his landmark publication of 1973, *Explaining Music*. Example 12-5 uses his graphing technique, which shows the implications of melodic patterns and their realizations in later melodic events. Eugene Narmour's later books have developed and adapted Meyer's ideas; see especially *The Analysis and Cognition of Basic Melodic Structures*.

4. "Denature" here has nothing to do with nature or "natural properties" of harmony. My borrowing is from biochemistry, where to denature a large molecule means to change its fundamental properties by altering its shape.

5. Gary W. Don explores a specific tension associated with overtone series in "Brilliant Colors Provocatively Mixed: Overtone Structures in the Music of Debussy," 65–66, 70. Here is a case whereby one might well want to adapt the dimensional technique to this particular quality of Debussy's music by adding an "overtone dimension" that tracks the changes in that harmonic aspect.

6. In fact, one can easily hear a great tonic pedal underlying the entire opening sequence given in example 12-7. I have not graphed it because it never changes, thus does not really constitute a rhythm within this example. It may, however, provide some background tension owing to harmonic independence.

EPILOGUE

1. For discussion of these matters see *Musical Languages*, chap. 2, and "The Concept of Musical Syntax."

BIBLIOGRAPHY

Arlin, Mary Irene. "Harmonic Rhythm in Selected Fugues from *The Well-Tempered Clavier*, Book I." M.M. thesis, Indiana University, 1965.

Berry, Wallace. *Structural Functions of Music*. Englewood Cliffs, NJ: Prentice-Hall, 1976.

Berz, William L. "Working Memory in Music: A Theoretical Model." *Music Perception* 12 (spring 1995): 353–364.

Brothers, Lester D. "On Music and Meditation in the Renaissance: Contemplative Prayer and Josquin's *Miserere*." *Journal of Musicological Research* 12 (1992): 157–187.

Butler, David. *The Musician's Guide to Perception and Cognition*. New York: Schirmer, Books, 1992.

Caplin, William. "Theories of Harmonic-Metric Relationships from Rameau to Riemann." Ph.D. diss., University of Chicago, 1981.

Carroll, David. *The Psychology of Language*. Monterey, CA: Brooks/Cole, 1986.

Clifton, Thomas. *Music as Heard: A Study in Applied Phenomenology*. New Haven: Yale University Press, 1983.

Crist, Stephen A. "Aria Forms in the Vocal Works of J. S. Bach, 1714–24." Ph.D. diss., Brandeis University, 1988.

Davis, Shelley. "Harmonic Rhythm in Mozart's Sonata Form." *Music Review* 27 (1966): 25–43.

Deutsch, Diana. "Octave Generalization and Tune Recognition." *Perception and Psychophysics* 11: 411–412.

Don, Gary W. "Brilliant Colors Provocatively Mixed: Overtone Structures in the Music of Debussy." *Music Theory Spectrum* 23, 1 (spring 2001): 61–73.

Dowling, W. Jay, and Dane Harwood. *Music Cognition*. New York: Academic Press, 1986.

Eigeldinger, Jean-Jacques. *Chopin: Pianist and Teacher as Seen by His Pupils*. Trans.

Naomi Shohet with Krysia Osostowicz and Roy Howat. Ed. Roy Howat. Cambridge, UK: Cambridge University Press, 1986.

Harvard Dictionary of Music. Ed. Willi Apel. Cambridge: Harvard University Press, 1944.

Hasty, Christopher F. *Meter as Rhythm.* New York: Oxford University Press, 1997.

LaRue, Jan. "Harmonic Rhythm in the Beethoven Symphonies." *Music Review* 18, 1 (1957): 9–20.

Leech-Wilkinson, Daniel. *Machaut's Mass: An Introduction.* Oxford: Clarendon Press, 1990.

Lerdahl, Fred. "Cognitive Constraints on Compositional Systems." In *Generative Processes in Music: The Psychology of Performance, Improvisation, and Composition,* ed. John Sloboda, 231–259. Oxford: Clarendon Press, 1988.

Lerdahl, Fred, and Ray Jackendoff. *A Generative Theory of Tonal Music.* Cambridge: MIT Press, 1983.

Lester, Joel. *Compositional Theory in the Eighteenth Century.* Cambridge: Harvard University Press, 1992.

———. *The Rhythms of Tonal Music.* Carbondale: Southern Illinois University Press, 1986.

Macey, Patrick Paul. "Josquin's 'Miserere Mei, Deus': Context, Structure, and Influence." Ph.D. diss., University of California, Berkeley, 1985.

Mattheson, Johann. *Der vollkommene Kapellmeister.* 1739. Trans. and ed. Ernest C. Harriss. Ann Arbor, MI: UMI Research Press, 1981.

Meyer, Leonard. *Emotion and Meaning in Music.* Chicago: University of Chicago Press, 1956.

———. *Explaining Music.* Chicago: University of Chicago Press, 1973.

Narmour, Eugene. *Beyond Schenkerism.* Chicago: University of Chicago Press, 1977.

———. *The Analysis and Cognition of Basic Melodic Structures.* Chicago: University of Chicago Press, 1990.

Pashler, Harold E. *The Psychology of Attention.* Cambridge: MIT Press, 1998.

Piston, Walter. *Harmony.* New York: Norton, 1941.

Riemann, Hugo. *Musikalische Syntaxis: Grundriss einer harmonischen Satzbildungslehre.* Leipzig: 1877.

———. *Vereinfachte Harmonielehre oder die Lehre von den tonalen Funktionen der Akkorde.* New York: 1893.

Schumann, Robert. "12 Etüden für Pianoforte von Friedrich Chopin. Werk 25." In *Gesammelte Schriften über Musik und Musiker.* Vol. 2. Ed. F. Gustav Jansen. 2 vols. Leipzig: 1891.

Sessions, Roger. *Harmonic Practice.* New York: Harcourt, Brace, 1951.

Stravinsky, Igor. *Poetics of Music in the Form of Six Lessons.* Trans. Arthur Knoedel and Ingolf Dahl. Cambridge: Harvard University Press, 1970.

Swain, Joseph P. "The Concept of Musical Syntax." *Musical Quarterly* 77, 2 (summer 1995): 285–308.

———. "Musical Communities and Music Perception." *Music Perception* 11, 3 (spring 1994): 307–320.

———. *Musical Languages.* New York: Norton, 1997.

———. "The Need for Limits in Hierarchical Theories of Music." *Music Perception* 4 (fall 1986): 121–148.

———. "Teaching Harmonic Rhythm." *Journal of Music Theory Pedagogy* 13 (2001),

Warren, Richard et al. "Melodic and Nonmelodic Sequences of Tones: Effects of Duration on Perception." *Music Perception* 8 (spring 1991): 277–290.

Yeston, Maury. *Stratification of Musical Rhythm*. New Haven: Yale University Press, 1976.

INDEX